CONTRIBUTORS

C000185284

Principal author	
Pottery	
Finds	Angela Wardle
Ceramic building material	Susan Pringle
Sculptured and architectural fragments	Tom Blagg
Glass	John Shepherd
Human remains	Bill White
Animal remains	Kevin Rielly
Botanical remains	John Giorgi
Illustrations	David Bentley, Andy Chopping, Maggie Cox, Jane Sandoe, Kikar Singh
Project management	Robin Densem, Gillian King, Dick Malt, Peter Rowsome, Barney Sloane, Tracy Wellman
Academic adviser	Jenny Hall
Academic editing	Peter Rowsome, Barney Sloane

CONTENTS

List of figures vi

List of tables vii

Abstract viii

Acknowledgements ix

Introduction 1   1

    1.1 Location and circumstances of fieldwork 1

    1.2 Geology and topography 1

    1.3 Archaeological and historical background 2

    1.4 Organisation of this report 2

    1.5 Textual and graphic conventions in this report . . . 4

The archaeological sequence 2   5

    2.1 Period 1: natural drift geology 5

    2.2 Period 2: early land use (c AD 50–120) 5

        Phase 1: establishment of Watling Street 5

        Phase 2: early roadside building 7

        Period 2 discussion 8

    2.3 Period 3: the development of the roadside cemetery

        (c AD 120–250) 9

        Phase 1: the temple and unenclosed cemetery 9

        Phase 2: walled cemeteries, a mausoleum and other

        burials 14

        Period 3 discussion 22

    2.4 Period 4: the late Roman cemetery (AD 250–400) . 24

    2.5 Period 5: post-Roman activity (AD 400+) 25

Aspects of the Roman roadside cemetery 3   26

    3.1 The cemetery population 26

    3.2 Funerary rites, burial practice and belief 27

        Cremation burials 27

        Inhumation burials 29

        Burial goods 29

    3.3 Architectural evidence for the structures 30

    3.4 The cemetery in its wider context 31

Catalogue of burials and associated finds 4   33

    4.1 The burials and associated finds 33

    4.2 Probable displaced burial goods 48

    4.3 Artefacts from non-burial contexts 51

Specialist reports **5** 53

    5.1 The late Roman pottery 53

    5.2 Building materials 57

    5.3 Sculptures and architectural fragments 61

    5.4 The human bones 63

    5.5 The animal bones 64

    5.6 The plant remains – a summary 65

French and German summaries **6** 67

Bibliography 70

Index 73

FIGURES

Fig 1   Site location 2

Fig 2   Areas of archaeological investigation within the site boundaries 3

Fig 3   Graphic conventions used in this report 4

Fig 4   Principal archaeological features, Period 2 Phase 1 6

Fig 5   North-west facing section through Road 1 and roadside ditches to its south-west 7

Fig 6   Principal archaeological features, Period 2 Phase 2 8

Fig 7   Building 1 showing the posthole clusters which supported the external walls 9

Fig 8   Principal archaeological features, Period 3 Phase 1 11

Fig 9   Building 2, the possible temple-mausoleum, and an associated well 12

Fig 10   Tazze and lamps recovered from burial 1, a bustum 13

Fig 11   Excavation of burial 2, a prone inhumation . . . 14

Fig 12   Cemetery structures S1–S3, Period 3 Phase 2 . . . 15

Fig 13   Structure 1, a walled cemetery enclosing robbed-out features 16

Fig 14   Detail within Structure 1 showing amphora <P30>, with a carved stone pine cone <A2> in the background and a moulded stone cornice <A3> to its right 17

Fig 15   Burial 8 within Structure 1 17

Fig 16   A ceramic tettina <P29>, thought to be a displaced burial good, found within Structure 1 . . 18

Fig 17   Mausoleum Structure 2, with the walled cemetery Structure 3 in the background and Road 1 to the right 18

Fig 18   Plan of the mausoleum at Stone, Faversham . . . 19

Fig 19   Period 3 Phase 2: burials in Open Area 4 outside the funerary structures S1–S3 20

Fig 20   Burial 22, a mother with a baby (burial 23) at her foot 21

Fig 21   Period 4 – late Roman features in Open Area 5 and continued use of Road 1 23

Fig 22   The late Roman roadside ditch with a quarry pit cut into its base 25

Fig 23   A reconstruction of the Period 3 mid 2nd-century funerary structures along the south-west side of Road 1 31

Fig 24   Plan of burial 1, a bustum, two of the tazze <P10> and <P13> and the eight pottery lamps <P1> – <P8> recovered from the fill of the bustum . . . 34

Fig 25   The picture lamps <P1> – <P4> recovered from burial 1 35

Fig 26   The plain lamps <P5> – <P8> recovered from burial 1 36

Fig 27   Plan of burial 2, a prone inhumation burial whose feet were truncated 37

Fig 28   Plan of burial 8, an inhumation burial, with illustrations of the glass vessel <G15> found with the pottery vessel <P17> 39

Fig 29   Plan of burial 14, an inhumation burial within a stone-lined cist that had been robbed 40

Fig 30   Plan of burial 17, an inhumation burial, laid on a bed of chalk and with pottery vessel <P19> . . . 41

Fig 31   Plan of burial 19, a prone inhumation burial – head truncated – and burial goods <P20> and <P21> 41

Fig 32   Plan of burial 22, a female inhumation burial, with a baby, burial 23, at her foot 42

Fig 33   Plan of burial 25, an inhumation burial packed with chalk 43

Fig 34   Plan of burial 26, an inhumation burial packed with chalk, and associated burial goods <G3> and <S5> 44

Fig 35   Glass vessels <G4>, <G6>, <G7>, <G8>, <G9>, <G12>, <G17> and <G21> 46

Fig 36   Plan of burial 29, an inhumation burial, with grave good <P24> 48

Fig 37   Pottery vessels <P25>, <P26>, <P31> and <P56>, glass vessels <G13>, <G20> and <G22>, and small finds <S7> and <S9> 49

Fig 38   Amphora <P30> found within Structure 1 51

Fig 39   Late Roman pottery vessels <P32> – <P43> recovered from the Period 4 roadside ditch Group 10 54

Fig 40   Late Roman pottery vessels <P44> – <P55> recovered from the Period 4 roadside ditch Group 10 55

Fig 41   Roman carved stone head <A1> possibly a river god 61

Fig 42   Roman carved stone pine-cone finial <A2> 62

Fig 43   Roman moulded stone cornice <A3> (with profile) 63

Fig 44   Roman moulded stone cornice <A4> (with profile) 63

TABLES

Table 1   Archaeological sites in the vicinity of 165 Great Dover Street 4

Table 2   Period 2 dating evidence 10

Table 3   Period 3 dating evidence 22

Table 4   Period 4 dating evidence 24

Table 5   Catalogue of inhumation and cremation burials. 52

Table 6   Summary of cremated human remains 52

Table 7   Late Roman pottery – raw data by fabric 56

Table 8   Late Roman pottery – raw data by form 56

Table 9   Late Roman pottery – raw data by ware 57

Table 10   Late Roman pottery – raw data by type 57

Table 11   Late Roman pottery – raw data by source . . . 57

Table 12   Roman pottery fabric codes 58

Table 13   Roman pottery form codes 58

Table 14   Roman pottery decoration codes 59

Table 15   Roman pottery ware codes 59

Table 16   Calculated stature of four adults 64

Table 17   Summary of some characteristics of the inhumation burials 64

ABSTRACT

Excavations in 1996 and 1997 at 165 Great Dover Street, Southwark (TQ 3275 7935) (MoL site code GDV96), uncovered important new evidence of burials and structures associated with a Roman roadside cemetery to the south-east of the settlement. Natural (OA1) was overlain by an extant Roman sequence that began with an external area and a 1st-century ditch (OA2) aligned north-west to south-east. The ditch probably served as a marker for a Roman road (R1) interpreted as part of Watling Street. A late 1st-century building (B1), whose external walls were set on piled foundations, was constructed on the south-west side of the road with its long axis perpendicular to the road alignment. The building measured at least 8.6m x 5m and respected a series of ditches on open land to either side (OA3) and which may have been part of a contemporary field system.

Building 1 was dismantled and the ditches infilled to make way for a cemetery which was established no later than the mid 2nd century. A masonry building (B2) measuring c 8m x 8m was located on the southern part of the main excavation area, set back from the road which lay to the east. The layout of the building suggests that it may have been a temple or temple-mausoleum, with a discontinuous outer wall around a central *cella* and an integral well or soakaway. The base for a possible altar was located between the inner and outer walls of the building, as were at least two inhumation burials.

A small number of inhumation burials lying c 30m to the north (OA4) may have been contemporary with Building 2. An associated *bustum* contained the cremated remains of a female with at least nine pottery tazze, eight pottery lamps and an exceptional array of plant remains, many imported from the Mediterranean, including stone pine, white almond and the first occurrence in London of date fruit. Images on the lamps included Anubis and a gladiator.

Three additional cemetery structures were built to the north of Building 2, and even closer to the roadside, between the mid 2nd and mid 3rd centuries. Walled cemetery S1 lay immediately to the north of Building 2 and was probably constructed while it was still in use. Structure 1, which measured c 11m x 9m, contained at least four burials and a centrally located, large masonry foundation which may have formed the base of a tomb or mausoleum. A smaller rubble foundation lay to the south of the central foundation and was probably the base of another monument. On the north side of the central foundation an amphora that had been buried upright and contained a deposit of nails was probably the receptacle of libations for the departed. A large cut located in the south-west corner of the enclosure contained an inhumation burial whose head had been removed and placed on the chest after the body had decayed. Rubble within the area of walled cemetery S1 included a carved stone pine cone and a moulded cornice, both thought to have come from one or other of the tombs. Structure 1 may have continued in use until sometime after the demolition of Building 2, and the outer wall of the wall cemetery was partially robbed in the mid 3rd century or later.

A possible mausoleum (S2) lay immediately to the north of walled cemetery S1 and may have either predated or postdated it. The mausoleum measured c 6m x 5.8m and had external buttresses on its north-west and south-east sides, suggesting that it may have had a vaulted roof, although no evidence of decoration survived.

A second walled cemetery (S3) lay further to the north and measured c 9m x 4m. This cemetery enclosure also had an outer wall around a centrally located mortared flint foundation, and contained four inhumation burials.

A number of inhumation and cremation burials were recorded outside the confines of the walled cemetery structures but were contemporary with their use and dated to between the mid 2nd and mid 3rd centuries. These included a cluster of three chalk-lined burials dated to the late 2nd to 3rd centuries and lying to the south-west of mausoleum structure S2.

The roadside cemetery, which was most extensive in the early 3rd century, indicates that construction of high-status mausolea and other burial structures extended about half a kilometre down Watling Street from the likely boundary of the settlement. The arrangement of the structures and lack of intercutting burials suggest that the cemetery held private plots used by wealthy families for extended periods of time.

The funerary structures had fallen into a state of disrepair by the late 3rd century, although there was some evidence that the area may have continued to be used as an unenclosed cemetery (OA5). In all a total of 25 inhumation burials and five cremation burials were recorded from all phases of the cemetery.

The road itself continued in use throughout the life of the cemetery and perhaps beyond it. A carved head of a bearded god, possibly a water deity, came from a late Roman roadside ditch. The roadside ditch was redug in the late 3rd century but had silted up again by the late 4th century.

Post-Roman activity was represented by pitting in the medieval period and in the 17th to 19th centuries. The most recent extant activity recorded on the site was related to the construction of various brick features including wells or soakaways, a cellar and other walls in the 19th century.

The excavation findings from Great Dover Street are a significant addition to our knowledge of Roman London's cemeteries and complement the major study into the Roman cemetery east of the main settlement (Barber & Bowsher 2000). The prime objective of the present volume is to describe the findings at Great Dover Street rather than to attempt a synthesis of Roman London's burial archaeology.

ACKNOWLEDGEMENTS

MoLAS would like to extend its sincere thanks to Nigel Scott and Robin Lackey of Berkeley College Homes Ltd which generously funded the excavation and post-excavation work. We would also like to thank Anne Thompson, Janet Miller and Anthony Martin of Gifford & Partners, the London Borough of Southwark Senior Archaeology Officer, successively John Dillon and Sarah Gibson, and Chris Pidcock of DMWR (Douglas Marriot Worby Robinson) Architects.

The author would like to express his thanks to all the MoLAS staff who worked on the site, and in particular Ryszard Bartkowiak, Ian Blair, Dick Bluer, Simon Cox, James Drummond-Murray, Stuart Gibson, Richard Heawood, Richard Hewett, Nick Holder, John Roberts, Nick Sambrook, Jez Taylor, Chris Tripp and Ken Pitt. Thanks are also due to Duncan Lees and Kate Pollard for surveying and Mark Samuel who offered initial comments on the worked stone.

Robin Densem helped with the project management of the project. Barney Sloane and Peter Rowsome provided post-excavation project management and advice on the form and content of the publication, as well as editorial assistance.

MoLAS would also like to thank Mark Hassall for comments on the graffiti and Jenny Hall, Barney Sloane and Peter Rowsome for their comments on the text. Tom Blagg, who provided valuable advice on the reconstruction drawing, passed away before he could see this publication. He will be missed by us all.

Angela Wardle is grateful to Donald Bailey for assistance in finding parallels for the Anubis lamps and for providing a copy of his unpublished report on the Mucking grave group.

Tom Blagg expressed his gratitude to Dr Martin Henig for his comments on the draft text of the bearded god, and to David Peacock and David Williams of the University of Southampton for identification of the stone for the bearded god and the pine-cone finial.

The index was compiled by Susanne Atkin, and the French and German summaries were written by Kay Cohen and Frederieke Hammer.

1

Introduction

1.1 Location and circumstances of fieldwork

The site, called 165 Great Dover Street, included 162–167 Great Dover Street (Ordnance Survey national grid reference TQ 3275 7935) in the London Borough of Southwark and was located c 1km south of the River Thames (Fig 1). The redevelopment area consisted of land bounded by Becket Street to the north, Tabard Street to the east, Black Horse Court to the south and Great Dover Street to the west. The land was occupied by a mixture of brick buildings. The largest, at 165 Great Dover Street, was built in 1897 and was formerly a post office. Post-war redevelopment along the Tabard Street and Black Horse Court frontages had removed all archaeological remains down to the level of the natural sand and gravel deposits, but the absence of basements in the north-west corner of the site and in several other areas had resulted in the survival of archaeological deposits.

The proposed redevelopment of the site by Berkeley College Homes Limited, to provide student accommodation for Guy's and St Thomas' Hospital Trust, entailed further basementing which would result in the destruction of much of the remaining volume of archaeological deposits. No archaeological work was necessary beneath 165 Great Dover Street, which was the subject of refurbishment only. Following a desktop assessment and the monitoring of machine-dug testpits by the developers' archaeological consultants Gifford & Partners, a need for further archaeological work was identified. The Museum of London Archaeology Service (MoLAS) was contracted to carry out this work between September and November of 1996.

The main excavation (Fig 2) in Area 1 took place in two phases, A and B, with a short phase of watching brief (WB1) further to the north-east on the Tabard Street frontage. At the same time ground reduction in other areas of the site (Areas C to H) where archaeology may have survived was monitored. Archaeological deposits were located only in Areas C, E and F surviving at c 2.0m OD. In Areas D, G and H existing double basements had removed any archaeological deposits. Following the main excavation there were further phases of archaeological work in 1997. To the south-east of Area 1 an area that had previously been inaccessible was investigated as WB2. Area C was later reduced to the level of natural gravels and this work was monitored as WB3. Finally in Area E the digging of a narrow pipe trench 23m long was monitored as WB4. Apart from this pipe trench the archaeological deposits found in Areas E and F were not disturbed, and these were preserved beneath a covering of terram and crushed concrete. The site is archived by the Museum of London under the site code GDV96.

1.2 Geology and topography

In the pre-Roman period much of north Southwark was made up of a series of low-lying sand islands or eyots rising above

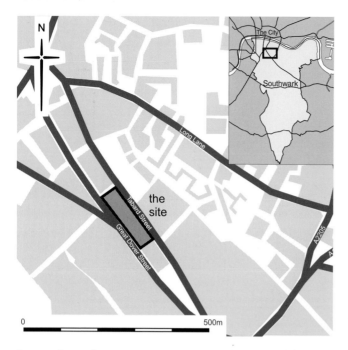

Fig 1 Site location © Crown copyright. All rights reserved. Corporation of London LA 087254/00/09

marshy land along the Thames. The location of the Roman bridge across the Thames was determined by Southwark's topography and lay very near to the site of the present-day London Bridge. The Roman bridge established the shortest crossing to Londinium from firm ground on the south bank of the river and which could be reached from the south by roads crossing the eyots. Subsequent Roman occupation and development in Southwark was concentrated on the larger of the islands.

The Great Dover Street site lay some distance to the south of the Thames and south-east of the Roman bridgehead, on the edge of Thames River terrace (or floodplain terrace) gravels and near the point where the post-glacial Thames has left an escarpment. A combination of windblown and waterlain silt deposits known colloquially as 'brickearth' cap the sands and gravels of the terrace. The course of Roman Watling Street followed the high ground south-east from the bridge and the Roman settlement in Southwark towards the Kent coast. Watling Street was thought to follow the course of Kent Street (now Tabard Street) and is known from excavations to follow the line of the Old Kent Road.

1.3 Archaeological and historical background

Evidence of prehistoric activity in the vicinity of Great Dover Street is very limited, with only a few struck flints and one possible fragment of pottery recorded, although the limited nature of the evidence may reflect the restricted research aims of previous investigations. The site lay outside the main core of Roman Southwark, which developed from c AD 50 onwards,

although it should be noted that no precise settlement boundary has been identified. The status and character of the Roman settlement south of the Thames is the subject of debate, with arguments for military and civilian origins, but the evidence continues to be inconclusive.

A number of previous archaeological investigations in the area of Great Dover Street have found evidence of Roman (and later) activity. These are summarised in Table 1.

Evidence of Roman inhumation burials and burial goods has been found in the area around Tabard Street in the past (Hall 1996). Antiquarian reports in the Royal Commission on Historical Monuments on Roman London (1928) refer to a loose cluster of cremation burials less than 300 yards to the south of the site, on Deverell Street, and at least three inhumation burials at Trinity Square about the same distance to the west (pl 55). Nearer to 165 Great Dover Street two inhumation burials of possible 4th-century date were reported to have been found in 1938 at the corner of Falmouth Road and Great Dover Street at a depth of about 6ft (Marsden 1961).

Recent work (Hall 1996) has summarised the evidence of Roman London's cemeteries and a major and detailed study of the burial practices from the eastern cemetery centred on Mansell Street, near Aldgate, has now been published (Barber & Bowsher 2000). Further synthesis of the Roman burials in Southwark is currently in preparation (Cowan et al in prep).

No evidence of Saxon activity has yet been found in the Great Dover Street area. Documentary evidence indicates that parts of the area were known as 'Horsemongerland' by 1290 (Canterbury Chapter Archives: Carta Antiqua W.76 – Stephen Humphrey, pers comm).

The area of the site was probably used for market gardens, smallholdings and horsemongering from about the 12th century onwards. On John Rocque's map of 1746 the site is shown as lying in an area of cultivated land behind houses along the Kent Street frontage and bisected by a linear, north-west to south-east aligned field boundary ditch. Horwood's map of 1813 shows the newly created Great Dover Street but little development alongside it. To the north-east on Kent Street there were more buildings and yards extending up to the field boundary ditch seen on the Rocque map.

The Ordnance Survey map of 1870 shows that the area of the present site had become heavily built up with houses, yards, a furniture warehouse and the Brunswick Methodist Chapel. In 1877 Kent Street became Tabard Street. Following bomb damage in the Second World War the area was heavily redeveloped, but there is no record of any archaeological work being undertaken on the site at that time.

1.4 Organisation of this report

This report forms part of the MoLAS Archaeology Studies series. The series is primarily intended to facilitate production of archaeological reports for the London region by working

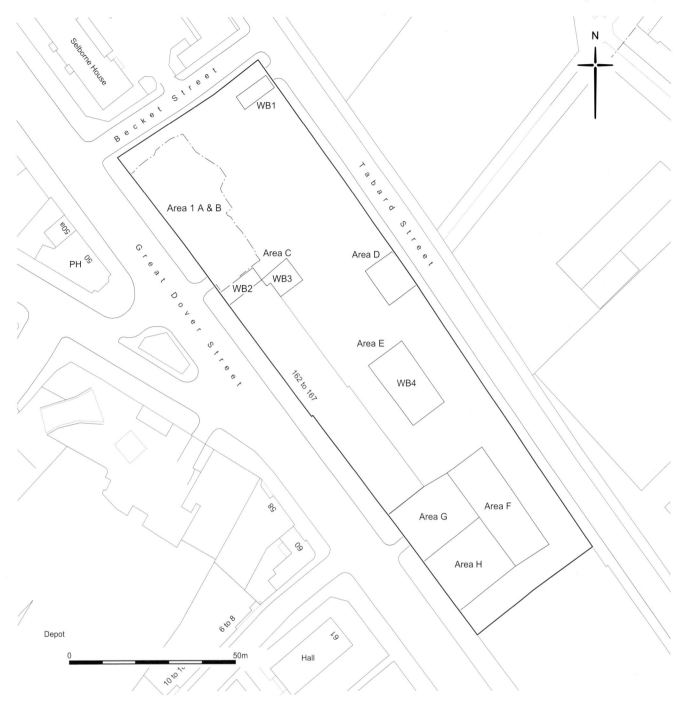

N

Becket Street

Selborne House

WB1

Great Dover Street

Area 1 A & B

50a

PH   50

Area C

WB2   WB3

162 to 167

Tabard Street

Area D

Area E

WB4

58

60

Area G

Area F

Area H

6 to 8

Depot

0   50m

10 to 1(

61

Hall

Fig 2 *Areas of archaeological investigation within the site boundaries* © *Crown copyright. All rights reserved. Corporation of London LA 087254/00/09*

closely in association with local and regional societies. The series aims to present smaller or medium-scale archaeological investigations, sometimes as single-site sequences and at other times with more than one site being linked by broad chronological or subject-matter themes. The series is further designed to link with the MoLAS Monograph series, through consistent use of format and design. MoLAS would welcome any comments on the design and content of this series.

The arrangement of each volume in the Studies series will follow a similar order, where, for each site involved, the circumstances of the investigation(s) precede a chronological narrative divided where appropriate by archaeological 'period' and land-use entities (Buildings, Open Areas, Roads and

Structures). A discussion section develops the analysis of the principal foci of the site(s) followed by pertinent supporting specialist reports.

In this report, the chronological sequence summarises the development of the cemetery, giving a precis of each of the burials (chapter 2), and is followed by discussions of aspects of the Romano-British cemetery (chapter 3). Detailed description and discussion of the burials and associated finds are presented in an illustrated catalogue, showing the location of the finds within the individual graves where appropriate (chapter 4). While this may appear repetitious, it is hoped that it will assist readers in gaining an overview of the whole site before attending to the specifics of the burials.

Table 1 Archaeological sites in the vicinity of 165 Great Dover Street

Site	Code	Location	Details
Swan Street, Great Dover Street	SS73	TQ 3247 7960	One struck flint was recovered. Two inhumation burials thought to be 4th century in date were cut into the side of a wide shallow ditch running north-east to south-west and which was infilled in the 3rd century.
Chaucer House, Tabard Street	CH75	TQ 3266 7962	A late 2nd-century inhumation was found cutting a ditch thought to be associated with the north side of Roman Watling Street. Three other ditches (two 2nd century and one 4th century) lay parallel to the course of the postulated road.
Rephidim Street	RS76	TQ 3290 7920	One fragment of possible prehistoric pottery was found. A 2nd-century ditch system lay adjacent to the course of Roman Watling Street. Further to the north was a silted-up stream channel.
Silvester Buildings, Silvester Street	SB76	TQ 3250 7970	Two struck flints and a core were found. Evidence of flooding in the early Roman period, a 1st-century pit, a late Roman well and medieval pitting were recorded.
Cardinal Bourne Street	CBS77	TQ 3238 7912	During the Roman period the area was waterlogged and was crossed by two streams. A gravel spread may have been a road.
Arcadia Buildings, Silvester Street, Great Dover Street	AB78	TQ 3257 7966	Residual flints were found. A prehistoric channel was overlain by a Roman road, with associated 1st- and early 2nd-century timber buildings and evidence of metalworking. In the 3rd century gravel was quarried from the road. In the 4th century the road was reinstated with new drains and roadside buildings. The Roman sequence was sealed by a 'dark earth' deposit, an 11th-/12th-century ditch, 15th- to 16th-century pits and a 17th-century brick building with a pipe kiln.

1.5 Textual and graphic conventions in this report

The basic unit of cross-reference throughout the archive that supports this report is the context number. This is a unique number given to each archaeological event on site (such as a layer, wall, pit cut, road surface etc). Context numbers in the text are normally shown thus: [100].

The archaeological sequence is expressed in terms of periods and land use. The periods are unique to the evidence from the site, and are based on a combination of artefactual dating and major stratigraphic development of the site. A particular period may be subdivided into phases.

This report employs the same Building, Open Area, Road and Structure numbers as are used in the archive report (sometimes here abbreviated B, OA, R and S) . These features are numbered sequentially through the excavated sequence, from the bottom up, and describe the history of the land use recorded on the site. Given the relative simplicity of the sequence, a land-use diagram has not been included. The land-use text and accompanying drawings showing development over time are of course an interpretation of the findings as excavated and do not necessarily describe

the complete, original structural history of the site or the only 'right' way of presenting it.

Accession numbers given to certain artefacts from the site are shown thus: <100>.

The graphic conventions used on the period and detail plans in this report are shown on Fig 3.

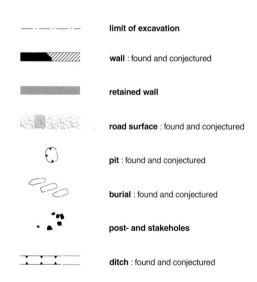

Fig 3 Graphic conventions used in this report

2

The archaeological sequence

2.1 Period 1: natural drift geology

Open Area 1: natural

The underlying geology at Great Dover Street consisted of Thames River terrace sand and gravel overlain by brickearth deposits that were laid down by a combination of wind and water action and date from the time of the last glaciation c 26,000 to 13,000 years ago. The surface of the sand and gravel sloped from c 1.3m OD at the north-west of the site to c 1.15m OD at the south-east, and consequently more undisturbed natural brickearth was found to the south-east. In several instances the brickearth contained thin bands of a white, almost chalky material.

2.2 Period 2: early land use (c AD 50–120)

Period 2 can be divided into two phases – the first being the laying out and construction of Roman Watling Street (R1) across open ground (OA2), and the second the construction of a timber building (B1) fronting on to the road and associated with a possible field system (OA3).

Phase 1: establishment of Watling Street

Open Area 2: open land and marking-out or boundary ditch

The earliest extant evidence of human activity recorded within Area 1 was a ditch which ran north-west to south-east for a distance of at least 40m, continuing beyond the limits of excavation (Fig 4). Five sections were excavated across the ditch and its width was found to vary from just over 1m to 1.5m, while its depth was between 0.5m and 0.6m. The ditch appeared to have been deliberately backfilled with fairly clean brickearth, suggesting that it was not open for any length of time. The ditch backfill can be dated from 1st-century and possibly pre-Flavian pottery, with such diagnostically early forms as Lyon Colour-coated ware (LYON), Highgate 'B' ware storage jars (HWB 2V), Colchester White ware early wall-sided mortaria (COLWW 7EWAL) and Early Roman Sandy B ware bead-rim jars (ERSB 2A15) present. Sherds dating to c AD 100–20 (context [182]) are thought to be intrusive in the upper part of the ditch fill.

It seems likely that the ditch was more than a field boundary as there was very little variation in its dimensions or in the material used to backfill it. The apparent regularity and short use of the ditch suggest a specialised function, and it may have marked out the course of the road which was parallel with it. Another possibility is that the ditch delineated

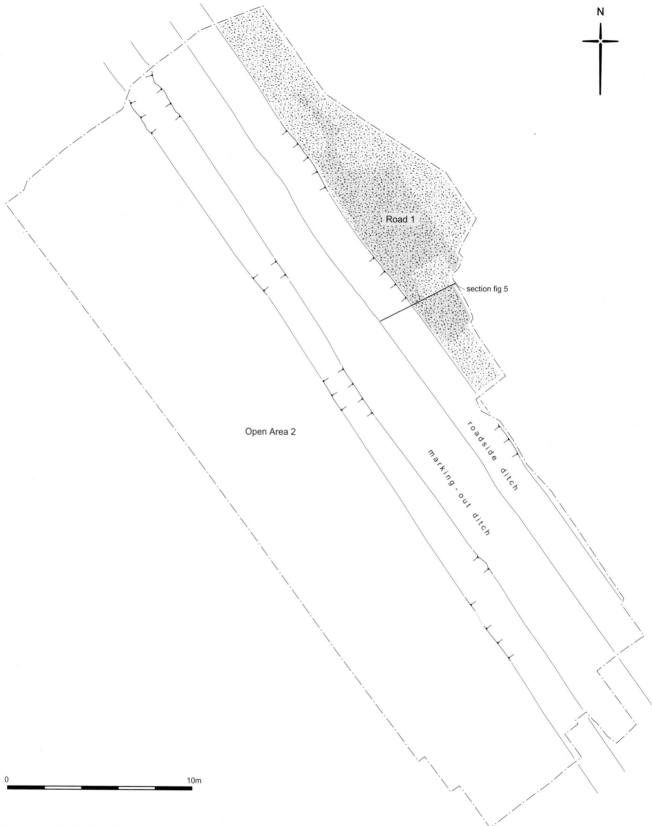

N

Road 1

section fig 5

Open Area 2

roadside ditch

marking - out ditch

0   10m

Fig 4 Principal archaeological features, Period 2 Phase 1

part of the boundary of an early burial area. Two fragments of large, square-sectioned glass vessels <G19> and <G20> recovered from the fill of the ditch were dated to the late 1st to 3rd centuries and may have originally functioned as cinerary urns (see 4.2 below).

Some of the external spreads situated to the south-west of

the ditch included disturbed brickearth deposits which may postdate the construction of Building 1 (see below) but could not be separated from earlier Open Area 2 deposits and are therefore included here. The spreads contained pottery dated to AD 50–160, 1st-century brick and roof tile in local and north-west Kent fabrics, a single large block of Kentish

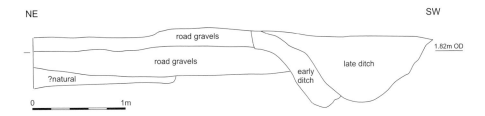

NE

SW

road gravels

road gravels

?natural

early
ditch

late ditch

1.82m OD

0   1m

Fig 5 North-west facing section through Road 1 and roadside ditches to its south-west

ragstone rubble and an *opus spicatum* brick of 2nd- to 3rd-century date in a rare fabric type 3005, probably from a Kentish source (see 5.2 below).

Road 1: Roman Watling Street

The north-west to south-east line of Road 1 was formalised by the laying of a metalled surface, perhaps shortly after the digging of the marking-out ditch in Open Area 2. The road metalling consisted of a series of gravel deposits laid directly over the natural brickearth and forming an agger running north-west to south-east (see Fig 4). Although truncated by later activity the gravels delineated the south-western edge to the road. The highest extant road gravel was at *c* 1.7m OD and the deposits were up to 0.5m thick. One of the lower gravel layers produced pottery dating to the late 1st to mid 2nd century.

An area of double basements to the north-east of Area 1 had removed any trace of the road, preventing an estimate of its original width. The top of Road 1 was truncated and sealed by a dark earth deposit containing post-Roman finds.

Along the south-western edge of Road 1 a ditch was recorded both in plan and section (Fig 5) in Area 1, and was also noted during the watching brief (WB3), although no road gravels survived in the latter area. The ditch was aligned north-west to south-east, parallel with the possible marking-out ditch in Open Area 2, and was presumably dug at about the same time that Road 1 was established. The roadside ditch remained open until at least the mid 2nd century.

Road 1 is probably a continuation of the road found at Arcadia Buildings (AB78) to the north-west. At Arcadia Buildings the road lay at *c* 2.3m OD and was *c* 6.60m wide in its later stages of use. It appeared to have experienced a period of poor maintenance or even disuse sometime after the 2nd century but to have been rebuilt in the 4th century. The road has been interpreted as the major Roman road known as Watling Street, which was established *c* AD 50 and ran from London to Dover.

Phase 2: early roadside building

Building 1: timber building

Following the infilling of the Open Area 2 marking-out ditch Building 1 was constructed to the south-west of Road 1 and its associated roadside ditch (Fig 6). The building only survived

as two parallel lines of postholes grouped in clusters of four (Fig 7). As found, the building measured 8.6m x 5m, with the long axis of the building aligned north-east to south-west, perpendicular to the road. It is possible that the building continued further to the south-west beyond the site limits.

The posthole clusters could have supported either timber sill beams up to 0.45–0.50m wide, or post pads for upright timbers. Mudbrick would probably have been used to form the walls. The only evidence of possible internal divisions was provided by traces of a burnt sill beam 0.2m wide perhaps representing a partition located 1.2m from and parallel to the south-east wall. A brickearth floor surface contained some late 1st-century pottery.

The disused postholes contained silt, suggesting that the building had been dismantled, rather than decaying *in situ*. The building appears to have had a relatively short lifespan, although the density of posthole clusters and width of the walls suggest that it was a robust, permanent structure.

Open Area 3: open land around Building 1

A number of cut features were recorded in Open Area 3 (see Fig 6), to both the north-west and south-east of Building 1. Running north-west to south-east and parallel with the roadside ditch were three lengths of ditches, at least two of which had butt ends showing that they did not run continuously. Another ditch ran south-west to north-east alongside the south-eastern edge of Building 1 but terminating some distance short of the roadside ditch. The appearance of all these ditches suggests that they were field boundaries. The ditches do not seem to have been open for any length of time, and went out of use at about the same time as Building 1 was dismantled. They were deliberately backfilled with brickearth, probably in the late 1st century or early 2nd century. One ditch contained a small amount of tile in north-west Kent fabric, which dates from *c* AD 50–80.

A vertically sided circular feature located 12m to the north-west of Building 1 was probably a well, although it was not possible to excavate the feature to its base to check if there were any structural remains. Several undated pits and a possible ditch were located to the south-east of Building 1 in watching brief area WB2. A circular wood-lined pit or well nearby was dated to the 1st century. Further to the south-east in watching brief area WB4 an infilled quarry pit was recorded.

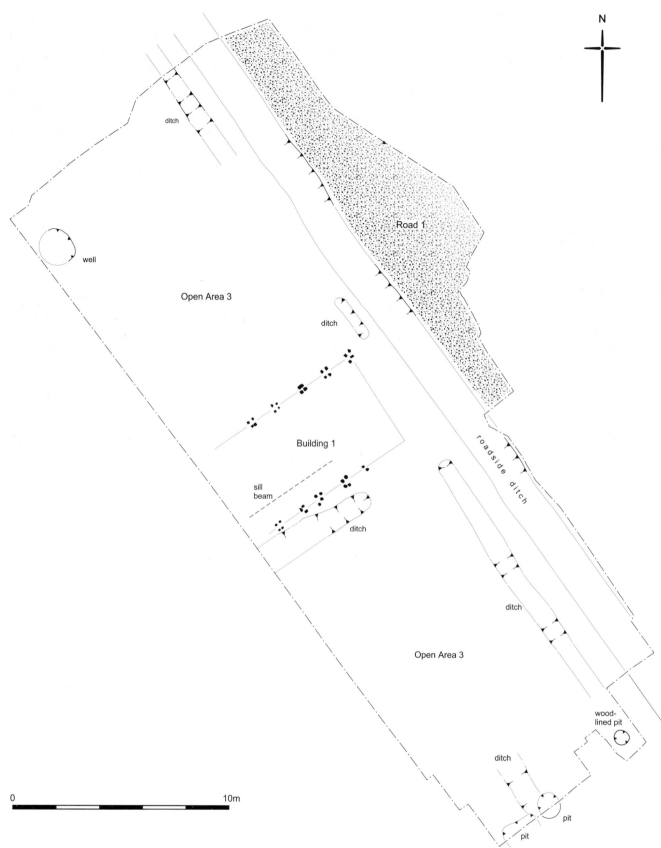

N

Fig 6 *Principal archaeological features, Period 2 Phase 2*

Period 2 discussion

(Table 2)
The evidence from the 165 Great Dover Street site is consistent with the view that Watling Street (Road 1) was laid out in the

1st century. A 1st-century ditch in the external area to the south-west (Open Area 2) may have served as a marker for the road and was parallel with it. Initial occupation, dated to the late 1st century, included an isolated roadside timber structure Building 1) set in an arrangement of fields and/or gardens

Fig 7 Building 1 viewed from the south-east, showing the posthole clusters which supported the external walls (scale 10 x 0.10m)

defined by ditches (Open Area 3). The apparent association between Building 1 and the adjacent ditches and fields may imply that the building was part of a farm, but this is far from certain. In any case the arrangement of building and fields did not last long. Building 1 was dismantled and the associated ditches deliberately backfilled, perhaps early in the 2nd century, to make way for an entirely different form of land use.

2.3 Period 3: the development of the roadside cemetery (c AD 120–250)

Period 3 includes the development of a roadside cemetery and the continued use of Road 1 and its roadside ditches. In Period 3 Phase 1 a small temple-like building (B2) with a possible ritual well was constructed in the southern part of Area 1, while an inhumation cemetery was established to the north (OA4). Period 3 Phase 2 includes the establishment of two walled cemeteries (Structure 1 and Structure 3) separated by a probable mausoleum (Structure 2), all lying to the north-west of Building 2. Although Building 2 was probably still in use when the adjacent walled cemetery S1 was built, it seems

to have gone out of use before the other structures and was partly robbed.

Inhumation and cremation burial continued to take place outside Structures 1–3 in Open Area 4. The evidence indicates that at least this section of Watling Street was lined with high-status, ornate tombs and monuments in roadside cemeteries from the mid 2nd century onwards.

Phase 1: the temple and unenclosed cemetery

Building 2: probable temple-mausoleum

A masonry building (B2) was recorded in the southern part of Area 1, set back from Road 1 and its roadside ditch. The ground plan was suggestive of a temple consisting of an inner structure or cella and an outer wall forming a precinct (Figs 8 and 9). The inner masonry walls formed a structure measuring 4.7m north-east to south-west by 4.2m north-west to south-east. Three of the walls survived only as foundations 0.5m– 0.8m wide, constructed of Kentish ragstone and Reigate stone. The foundations enclosed an area of just over 3m square, with the north-eastern side partly robbed out. No associated features were found within the area enclosed by the foundations. To the north-west was a partly robbed, stone-lined well 0.80m in diameter and with a base at 0.00m OD. The well appeared to

9

Table 2 Period 2 dating evidence (AD 50–120)

Activity	Grp	Sbgrp	Description	Date range
Open Area 2: open land and marking-out ditch to SW of Road 1				
External deposit	2	206	AHSU; BAETE 8DR20; GAUL 8; GROG 2T, 5; HWB 2A1-4; OXID 9LA <3>	AD 50–100
External deposit	2	2010	BAETE 8DR20; ERSB 2A15; FMIC 3 BDD; GAUL1 8G; NKSH	AD 60–100
Backfill marker ditch	3	306	AHSU; BAETE 8DR20; ERSB 2A15; FMIC; HWB; RWS; SAMLG 5DR15/17; SAND 2A; VRW	AD 60–100
Backfill marker ditch	3	3011	BAETE 8DR20PW11; LYON RCD1	AD 50–70
Comments: 2/206 8 of 16 sherds grog-tempered including a dish which has a carinated wall with internal moulding which suggests a mid 1st-century date.				
Building 1: timber building perpendicular to Road 1				
Occ layer	12	404	BAETE 8DR20; HWB; VCWS 2K; VRG	AD 70–100
Comments: Dated on VCWS.				
Open Area 3: open land to either side of Building 1				
Fill of pit or well	4	403	HWB 2A1-4; SAMLG; VRW 7HOF	AD 50–100
Field ditch	4	408	COLWW 7EWAL; VRW 1	AD 50–70

have been built as an integral part of the northern corner of the cella. Although the upper part of the well was robbed, it was clearly constructed of Kentish ragstone and included two large, rough-hewn pieces of Reigate stone rubble.

Surrounding the cella structure on three sides was an outer wall that was not continuous. To the north-west the wall survived as a masonry foundation while the north-eastern and south-western sides were robbed. It is possible there was a fourth wall to the south-west but if so this would have lain outside the limit of excavation. Located between the inner and outer walls along the south side of the building was a masonry feature which measured c 0.8m x 0.9m in plan and may have been the base of a small monument such as an altar.

A small pottery assemblage from the well was dated to the later 1st century, while the upper fill [354] was dated by one sherd of Cologne Colour-coated ware (KOLN) to the early 2nd century. Vessel links exist between sherds from the upper fill and a brickearth deposit [234] in Open Area 2, suggesting that the upper fills of the well were derived from or comprised of dumps of material obtained by excavation in the open land outside the temple. There were no obvious 'ritual' aspects to the pottery assemblage from the well. The backfill also contained a small ceramic building material assemblage. The assemblage included brick and roof tile fragments in local red fabrics (2815 fabric group), and a fragment of roof tile in a white fabric made in north-west Kent. Both tile types are typical of 1st-century assemblages. One brick fragment in non-local fabric 3019 is usually dated in London to the beginning of the 2nd century. Another small brick in fabric 3006 was worn on one long side, showing that it had been used in an opus spicatum floor. Such floors are usually associated with high-status, and particularly public, buildings.

Building 2 was similar in plan to many Romano-Celtic temples from north-west Europe. The incorporation of a well in the structure and the discontinuous outer wall are, however, unique in such structures. The outer wall could have formed an ambulatory, from 1m to 1.5m wide and possibly tiled, around the cella. Overall the building was quite small, measuring c 8m square. The cella is large enough to have permitted the placement of one or more stone or lead coffins and it may have functioned as a temple-mausoleum. The robbing of both walls

on the north-east side may be the result of an attempt to gain access to remove the contents of the cella. The associated well might have had a ritual function, although the finds do not suggest this.

No evidence of the internal or external decoration of the building was found, other than the small opus spicatum brick which may have been associated with it. Access to the building was probably from the road to the north-east where the land between the road and building was apparently open. There may have been a porch or steps leading to the cella, and the outer wall was not continuous, perhaps allowing access to the well head and possible altar. The roof of the building was probably tiled and in the reconstruction (see cover and Fig 23) the building is shown with an open ambulatory. A late 1st- to mid 2nd-century date, similar to that from the well, was obtained from a demolition deposit sealing the robbed north-east inner and outer walls. The latter contained one fragment of ceramic tile in a local red fabric (2815) dating to c AD 50–160. The robbed outer wall cut the previously infilled marking-out ditch, itself of a similar date.

A group of burials apparently interred inside the postulated outer wall of the temple were dated to after the late 1st or early 2nd century (see [b6] and [b7] below).

Open Area 4: burials

An open area (OA4) to the north-west of Building 2 apparently formed part of an unenclosed roadside cemetery and contained a bustum [b1] and four other burials dating to after the late 1st or early 2nd century. These burials and the possible temple (B2) can be associated only by their broad similarity of date, and not stratigraphically, although it is possible that the two burials lying inside the outer wall of the temple may have postdated it.

Burial [b1]: a bustum

Burial [b1] (see Fig 8; see also Fig 24 for detail) was a bustum, a rectangular pit dug beneath a cremation pyre to aid combustion, and then employed as a site of burial of the cremated remains. The pit cut was 0.8m wide and over 1m long; however, its location and the site conditions prevented

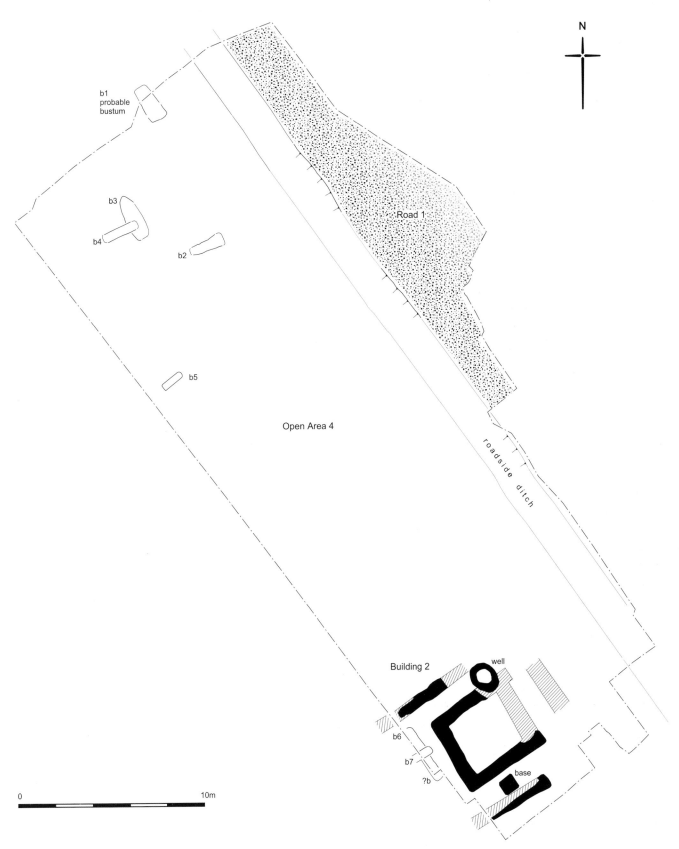

N

Fig 8 Principal archaeological features, Period 3 Phase 1

its full excavation. The sides were not scorched although fragments of burnt brickearth were found in the pit. Around at least one edge were several stakeholes which may represent stakes employed to help stabilise the pyre.

Excavation of the feature and examination of some 70 litres of soil samples revealed an exceptional array of plant remains, calcined bone and deliberately placed artefacts, which are summarised below. A more detailed analysis of the environmental remains will be published elsewhere (Giorgi *et al* in prep).

The charred plant assemblages consisted mainly of hundreds of unopened stone pine (*Pinus pinea*) nut shells, although some of the shells had broken open, and charred seeds of the species were also found. The presence of this plant was also confirmed by the identification of a large number of pine scales (over one hundred) which make up the cone as well as what appears to be the central stem of the cone stripped of both the scales and nuts. A particularly interesting find was of a virtually complete date (*Phoenix dactylifera*) fruit with the seed partially exposed; another possible fragment of this fruit was also identified. Several partially preserved fruits of fig (*Ficus carica*) together with loose seeds of this species were also found, while almond (*Prunus dulcis*) was also identified by a single nut. A large number of cereal grains were also present in the sample consisting mainly of six-row hulled barley (*Hordeum sativum*) and wheats (*Triticum* spp), which included the glume wheat, spelt (*T spelta*) and free-threshing bread wheat (*T aestivum*). Small fragments of charcoal were also identified in the sample.

Other biological remains in the sample included burnt (calcined) human and animal bone with the latter including the likelihood of a virtually complete adult chicken, with the femur and tibia estimated to have been heated to between 550° and 700°C (Alan Pipe, pers comm). The proximal end of a metatarsal from a small corvid (crow-type bird) was also identified.

The ritual represented here may have involved the placement of the 'raw' materials of a fine meal (pine cones, dates, figs, almonds, cereal grains and butchered chicken) – rather than the prepared dishes themselves – on to the funeral *bustum*. After charring slowly because they were away from the main focus of the fire, or smothered immediately after being placed in the fire, they rolled or were dropped into the pit below the pyre.

Eight ceramic lamps and eight tazze were recovered from the fill of the *bustum* (Fig 10; see also Figs 24–6). Due to time constraints the pit was not fully excavated and it is likely that more finds may have been present. The lamps were all made in the same fabric, Central Gaulish White ware, and of similar late 1st- to 2nd-century date. None of the lamps bears traces of sooting and they do not therefore appear to have been used. Four are 'picture lamps' (see Fig 25), and the choice of subject for the discus scenes appears to be deliberate. One (<P1>) shows a fallen gladiator, a relatively common type on the Continent, and the other three show jackal-headed Anubis, the Egyptian god of judgement who controlled entry to the underworld. This is a rare subject in Roman Britain and appears to be particularly suited to a funerary context. Whether the subject matter of the gladiator lamp can be taken as a clue to the identity of the cremated person can only be a matter of conjecture, but it is certain that the lamps were carefully chosen, together with the tazze which also

Fig 9 Building 2, the possible temple-mausoleum, and an associated well viewed from the south-east. Note that the small rectangular feature just beyond the scale and to the south-west of the well is post-medieval (scale 10 x 0.10m)

Fig 10 *Tazze and lamps recovered from burial 1, a bustum*

have a ritual significance being used as incense burners. The rest of the lamps are undecorated factory-made lamps, *Firmalampen* (see Fig 26), all of the same type although differing in the quality of the moulding and colour of the slip.

It may be significant that none of the lamps appears to have been used. They were perhaps provided for the ceremony and were intended to provide light in the underworld. Two of the Anubis lamps were broken, one (<P4>) so badly, that it was originally thought to be two separate objects. It is not certain whether the lamps were broken in antiquity as part of the ritual or as a result of post-burial damage, but the fact that only two were badly damaged makes the latter option more probable. It is however certain that the lamps and the tazze were placed in the cremation pit after the pyre had been extinguished as none is burnt. Molten glass was found in the cremation pit residues, indicating that glass vessels, perhaps containing unguents, were burned with the body as pyre goods. Iron nails were also found, perhaps deriving from a burnt coffin or other container.

Burial [b1] was a cremation, of an adult female, most of the bone appearing to come from the area of an upturned tazza. This suggests these cremated remains were gathered up (possibly even from another location) and added to this pit, reusing the original *bustum*. Excavated examples of *busta* are more common on the Continent (Barber & Bowsher 2000).

The *bustum* pit cut the similarly dated backfill of the marking-out ditch (see 2.2 Open Area 2 above). Some small fragments of north-west Kent tile were recovered from the backfill.

Other burials

Burial [b2] (Fig 11; see Fig 27 for detail) was a male aged 17 to 25 years, placed in a hastily prepared cut and with little ceremony: there was no proper grave cut or evidence of a coffin, the body was prone and one arm was outstretched – indicative of little care being employed. A fragment of glass <G2> from a Roman glass vessel of indeterminate form was recovered from the grave fill.

Burial [b3] was an adult, probably a female, laid north-west to south-east. Although only the upper leg bones were found, the body can be assumed to be an extended supine burial. There was no evidence of a coffin. The backfill contained finds dated to the 1st or 2nd century and fragments of north-west Kent brick.

The fourth burial [b4] was a male aged 26 to 45 years laid north-east to south-west with the head at the south-west. It was an extended supine burial with no evidence of a coffin and the hands joined over the pelvis. The backfill contained finds dated to the 1st or 2nd century and a fragment of fine *opus signinum* mortar with red-painted or skimmed surface. The leg bones of

Fig 11 Excavation of burial 2, a prone inhumation, viewed from the north-east

a young adult were also found in the backfill, suggesting that some disturbance of earlier graves had occurred.

The fifth burial [b5] was a child aged under 6 years laid north-east to south-west with the head to the south-west. It was also an extended supine burial but in a wooden coffin. The backfill contained finds dated to the 1st or 2nd century.

Two fragmentary burials were found to the south-east, between the south-west cella wall of the probable temple B2 and the limit of excavation. One burial [b6] was heavily truncated with only an arm bone remaining, lying in a north-west to south-east cut. It was truncated by the second burial [b7], which was also heavily truncated and only the legs were recovered. Burial [b7] was an extended supine burial aligned north-east to south-west. There was no evidence of a coffin although some crushed chalk was noted around the legs. Another nearby cut on a similar alignment to [b6] contained some nails and a fragment of glass and may have been a further grave cut.

Fills of both burial [b6] and burial [b7] contained pottery dating to the late 1st or 2nd century, as well as fragments of ragstone rubble.

Phase 2: walled cemeteries, a mausoleum and other burials

Structure 1: a walled cemetery

A rectangular enclosure measuring c 11m north-west to south-east by 9.2m north-east to south-west was created by the construction of a substantial masonry wall (Figs 12 and 13). The wall was made of Kentish ragstone and varied from 0.7m to 0.9m in width. The south-eastern wall was constructed hard up against the adjacent wall of Building 2, the possible temple, and it seems probable that the enclosure was formed while the temple was still in use. No trace of an entrance way to Structure 1 was found but access was probably from the south-west side. The enclosure evidently formed a walled cemetery and contained a number of masonry structures.

A large robbed-out masonry structure measuring 4.5m x 4.2m and 0.55m high lay in the centre of the enclosure. A section of masonry 1.35m x 0.8m and 0.26m high was found near the south-west corner of this feature and may have formed part of a wall built to surround the central portion of the structure, although the apparent loose nature of the masonry may rule this interpretation out. The whole of the central structure appears to have been some form of platform, perhaps the foundation for a mausoleum or similar monument. A fragment of natural green-blue Roman window glass <G23> was retrieved from the robbing debris.

An amphora [304] (Fig 14; see also Fig 38 and 4.3 below) was found 0.5m to the north-west of the platform, buried in an upright position. It is possible that the neck of the amphora originally protruded above the ground surface, as part of the handle was recovered from within the vessel top. The amphora contained an organic deposit which included a number of iron nails. There was no evidence of any cremated bone and the amphora may have acted as a receptacle for libations made by the living to the dead.

The top of the cut into which the amphora had been placed was sealed by a rubble deposit that included a carved stone pine cone and a fragment of cornice moulding (the carved pieces are dealt with in more detail in the period discussion below, and in 5.3). Ceramic building material included abraded early Roman brick (principally parts of three bricks in north-west Kent fabric) and roof tile. The rubble may have derived from the demolition of structures within the walled cemetery S1. It is also possible that there had once been some kind of superstructure over the amphora.

Some 0.5m to the south-east of the Structure 1 central platform was a vertical cut measuring 1.6m x 1.4m in plan and 0.8m deep. The cut was filled with fragments of Kentish ragstone, and early Roman brick and roof tile, and may have served as the base for a monument requiring a substantial foundation, such as a column or cenotaph.

In the south-west corner of the walled cemetery structure there was an unusual example of an inhumation burial [b8] which comprised two grave cuts, the larger one (see Fig 12) directly overlying a smaller one. The south-east side of each

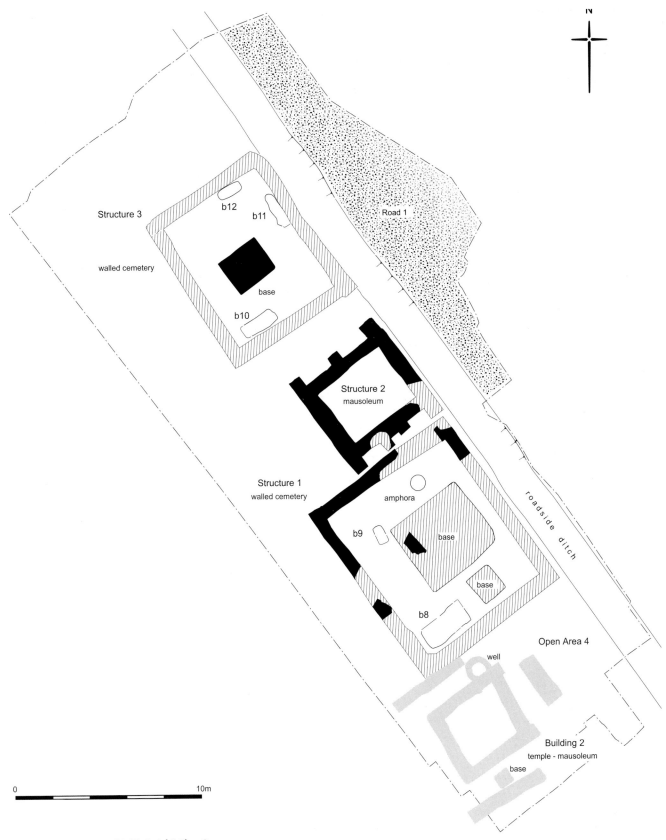

Fig 12 *Cemetery structures S1–S3, Period 3 Phase 2*

cut coincided precisely. The backfill of the earlier cut contained fragments of disarticulated bone, early Roman brick and roof tile, some of which was sooted, and an antler 'toggle'.

The later cut measured 2.7m x 1.3m, a particularly generous size for a grave. Occupying the south-east side of

the grave was the extended supine inhumation burial [b8] (Fig 15; see Fig 28 for detail). The individual was an adult male aged 26–45 years, whose skull (except the lower mandible) had been removed after tissue decay and placed on the chest. The inhumation burial was dated to after *c* AD 140

15

Fig 13 Structure 1, a walled cemetery enclosing robbed-out features, viewed from the south-east

by ceramic burial goods.

One interpretation of the [b8] sequence is that an earlier inhumation had been exhumed, leaving only fragmentary disarticulated bones. A new, larger grave was then dug, and another body [b8] laid to rest. Perhaps this burial location was for some reason particularly desirable.

Another inhumation burial within the walls of Structure 1 was that of a child under 6 years of age [b9] who had been buried extended and supine in a wooden coffin, with the head to the north-west. The burial was aligned north-west to south-east and was dated to the mid 2nd century.

A tettina (<P29> <10> [333]) (Fig 16) was found in the south-west corner of the enclosure and may have originally been a burial good that was later displaced (see 4.2 below).

The dating from the various features and burials within the enclosure, although limited, suggests that the Structure 1 walled cemetery was in use from about the mid 2nd century onwards.

Structure 2: a possible mausoleum

Immediately adjacent to the north-west side of the walled cemetery S1 was a ragstone masonry structure (S2), interpreted as a possible mausoleum (see Figs 12 and 17). The structure measured 6m north-west to south-east and 5.8m north-east to south-west. The walls survived as foundations constructed of

Kentish ragstone and occasional fragments of Reigate stone and were between 0.8m and 1m wide with small external buttresses at the corners of the north-west and south-east sides. Another buttress was located at the centre of the north-west side, and the central part of the south-east side featured two additional buttresses. The extra buttressing of the south-east side may have been necessary because that part of the mausoleum was built over an infilled ditch which may have been prone to subsidence. Alternatively these buttresses may mark the location of a small entrance. If so, the mausoleum S2 would have to have existed before the construction of the adjacent walled cemetery S1.

The width and depth of the foundations of Structure 2 suggest that it was a substantial structure, probably roofed, and the buttresses may have supported external pilasters to strengthen the walls. The ceiling of the structure may have been vaulted and a fragment of calcareous tufa found in a nearby backfilled timber well could have derived from it. No other evidence of internal or external decoration survived but the S2 ground plan is very similar to that of a mausoleum found at Stone-by-Faversham, Kent (Detsicas 1983) (Fig 18), and which had an *opus signinum* floor.

No burials were found within the area of Structure 2, and it may have functioned as a mausoleum building holding one or more sarcophagi, or even cremation vessels in niches. There were no datable artefacts found within the structure

Fig 14 Detail within Structure 1 showing amphora <P30>, with a carved stone pine cone <A2> in the background and a moulded stone cornice <A3> to its right (see Figs 38, 42 and 43). The linear structure in the top right-hand corner is modern (scale 2 x 0.10m)

Fig 15 Burial 8 within Structure 1, viewed from the south-east. The skull had been placed on the chest in antiquity. The truncation of the lower legs and damage to the skull is modern (scale 5 x 0.10m)

Fig 16 *A ceramic tettina <P29>, thought to be a displaced burial good, found within Structure 1*

but it must be later than the late 1st to early 2nd centuries as it cut a ditch infilled by that date. It is unclear how long the mausoleum may have been in use. An attempt had been made to rob the Structure 2 foundations in three separate, small areas, and the structure was eventually sealed by post-medieval dark earth deposits.

Structure 3: a walled cemetery

To the north of mausoleum S2 lay a second walled cemetery, Structure 3 (see Figs 12 and 17). The enclosure measured 9m north-west to south-east by 7m north-east to south-west, with an outer wall constructed of masonry and approximately 0.70m wide but completely robbed out. No evidence of an entrance way was found, but one may have existed in the middle of either the south-west or the south-east wall. At the centre of the enclosure was a plinth constructed of mortar and flint which measured 2.4m x 2.1m and at least 1.5m deep, interpreted as the base for either a funeral monument or a stone sarcophagus. The depth of the plinth suggests that it was able to support a substantial weight. Several fragments of *opus signinum* flooring were found in the post-medieval dark earth deposits directly overlying the plinth, and it may have been surfaced or finished in this material. In the north corner of Structure 3 there were a large number of undated stakeholes

and a few small postholes which cut into the brickearth and were for the most part sealed by post-medieval soils. Given that the stakes and posts were found only in one corner of the walled cemetery, with at least one cut by a burial, it seems likely that they represent the remains of some wooden structure set in a corner of Structure 3.

Within the enclosure walls and around the central plinth of Structure 3 were three inhumation burials, each located against one of the enclosure walls. Burial [b10] was a young child, under 6 years of age, in a wooden coffin and laid extended and supine in a north-east to south-west alignment. The bones of the lower body showed signs of disturbance. Another, older child [b11], aged 6 to 12 years was also buried extended and supine in a wooden coffin, laid north-west to south-east with the head to the north-west. The third burial [b12] was an extended supine adult female, laid north-east to south-west in a wooden coffin, with the head to the south-west. The upper body bones of [b12] were very disturbed and the lower leg bones had been moved and placed alongside the upper legs, suggesting reburial in antiquity. It seems plausible

Fig 17 *Mausoleum Structure 2 viewed from the south-east, with the walled cemetery Structure 3 in the background and Road 1 to the right. Chalk burials 25 and 27 can be seen to the left of Structure 2 (scale 10 x 0.10m)*

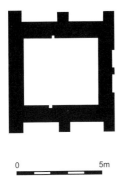

Fig 18 Plan of the mausoleum at Stone, Faversham (from Detsicas 1983), for comparison with Structure 2

that these individuals were members of one family, although no non-metric data were recorded from the skeletons to support this hypothesis.

There were no complete ceramic vessels that could be positively interpreted as burial goods associated with the Structure 3 burials, although the backfills of [b11] and [b12] did contain several joining large sherds. Overall the pottery from this area can be dated c AD 140–200. This date is supported by the absence of the late fine ware, Nene Valley Colour-coated ware (NVCC), which first appears in small quantities in London and Southwark during the later 2nd century but is more diagnostic of the 3rd century and is seen as a key indicator for assemblages dating to this period. Burial [b10] may have been a little later in date, as a later tegula was recovered from the backfill. While tile in this non-local fabric was appearing in London from the mid 2nd century onwards, it was more common in the 3rd century. Flakes of tile were present in all three burials, perhaps indicating that some activity involving either demolition or reworking of tile had taken place before the graves were filled in. Fragments of opus signinum plaster with pale and deep pink skims – probably from walls, ceilings, or funerary monuments – were also present. A coin of Hadrian (AD 117–38) was also found directly above the plinth.

It is possible that further burials had also taken place inside Structure 3, as two large post-medieval pits had removed all but traces of two further cuts [225] and [266], although no human bone was recovered from either. A small amount of local brick and tile, and four fragments of fine opus signinum mortar, one with fine and coarse layers, were retrieved from the pit backfills.

Open Area 4: burials outside Structures 1–3

Sixteen additional burials dated to the mid 2nd century onwards were found outside the walls of structures S1 to S3 (Fig 19). Fourteen of the burials were inhumations and two were cremations. Most of the burials appear to have postdated the construction of the walled cemeteries and the mausoleum. None was truncated by either walls or robbing cuts and some of these burials were clearly laid parallel to existing walls,

indicating that they were almost certainly contemporary.

The burials

Burial [b13] was a cremation of an adult of indeterminate sex, placed in a pottery vessel and buried upright. An adolescent [b14] (see Fig 29 for detail) was laid with the head to the north-west. The burial was extended and supine and was laid on a thin bed of gravel and sealed by loose fragments of ragstone and tile. Along one side of the grave cut was a fragment of ragstone wall suggesting there was originally around the body some sort of structure or lining that had been robbed. Fragments of early Roman roof tile, flue tile and brick dated to the mid 2nd century were found associated with the burial and may have come from the robbed lining. Burial [b15] was a child under 6 years of age and of indeterminate sex, laid in a wooden coffin. The bones were so scattered within the grave that the position of the head could not be determined. The burial contained finds dated to the mid 2nd century. These burials lay to the north-west of the location of walled cemetery Structure 3.

To the west of Structure 3 burial [b16] was an extended and supine adult female with the head to the south-west and no evidence of a coffin. Hobnails from shoes were recovered from the immediate vicinity of the burial, and as the feet and head were truncated by later activity, the shoes must have been laid alongside or on the torso. Burial [b16] also contained finds dated to the mid 2nd century. Nearby burial [b17] (see Fig 30 for detail) was an extended supine adolescent laid with the head to the south-west. The body had been placed on a bed of chalk in a wooden coffin with the hands joined over the pelvis. A pottery vessel from the grave was dated to AD 150–250. Burial [b18] was an extended supine adult male laid with the head to the north-west. There were no fittings to suggest the presence of a coffin. A small pit located nearby contained a pair of hobnailed shoes which were recorded on site but could not be recovered. The burial could not be dated, but was stratigraphically later than [b17].

To the south-west of Structure 2 burial [b19] (see Fig 31 for detail) was a prone young adult female laid with the head to the south-east. There was no evidence of a coffin. Two pots had been placed at the feet of the body and the burial was dated to the mid 2nd century or later. Burial [b20] was an extended supine adult of indeterminate sex aged 26 to 45 years with the head to the north-west. There was no evidence of a coffin. The burial cut into the fill of [b19], dating it to the mid 2nd century or later.

Further to the south-east and adjacent to the south-west corner of Structure 1, burial [b21] was a prone adult of indeterminate sex laid north-east to south-west and heavily truncated, with only the upper legs surviving. The burial may have been in a wooden coffin and was furnished with pottery and glass burial goods enabling it to be dated to the mid 2nd century or later. Burial [b21] partly cut through an earlier burial [b22] (Fig 20; see Fig 32 for detail), an extended supine female aged 17 to 25 years laid with the head to the south-east. There was no evidence of a coffin. The grave also contained a

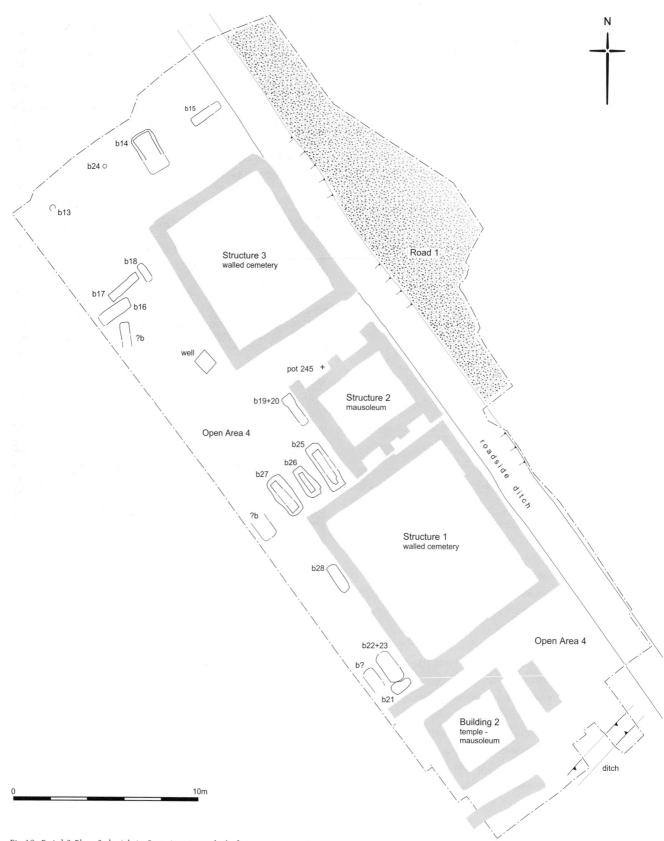

Fig 19 Period 3 Phase 2: burials in Open Area 4 outside the funerary structures S1–S3

neonate [b23], found in a foetal position partly under the right foot of [b22]. Several pottery fragments within [b22] were dated to AD 50–160; however, the burial is more likely to date to sometime after the mid 2nd century due to its alignment with the nearby walled cemetery S1 and its

stratigraphic relationship to [b21].

Burial [b24] was a cremation of an adult male placed in a pottery vessel buried upright and dating from the mid 2nd century, located between burials [b13] and [b14] at the northern end of the area.

A group of three burials [b25], [b26] and [b27] to the south-west of the Structure 2 mausoleum had all been placed in wooden coffins packed with a white substance and deposited in large grave cuts. Burials found with this type of packing have previously been referred to as 'plaster' burials. However, analysis by the Ancient Monuments Laboratory of similar deposits from burials in the Roman London eastern cemetery have found the principal constituent to be chalk (Barber & Bowsher 2000). Chalk may have been added in a liquid or powder form. Although often thought of as an aid to speed up decay, the purpose of such a packing is still debatable. The cluster of burials all using a similar burial rite is suggestive of a family grouping. Burial [b25] (see Fig 33 for detail) was a male aged 17 to 25 years laid with the head to the north-west. A glass disc was recovered from the grave fill and the burial was dated to the late 2nd or 3rd century. Burial [b26] (see Fig 34 for detail) was a child aged 6 to 12 years laid with the head to the south-east. This burial contained finds dated to the late 2nd or 3rd century. A broken jet pin was found near the feet and may have been used as a shroud pin. Burial goods, comprising a pair of shoes, a glass vessel and a chicken skeleton had been placed outside the foot end of the coffin and within the grave cut. Some large nails were noted around the edge of the grave cut suggesting there was an outer wooden structure, perhaps shuttering to hold open the grave sides during the act of burial. The size of the other two grave cuts may indicate that similar shuttering was used even though no nails were recovered. Burial [b27] was a female aged 26 to 45 years, laid with the head to the south-east. There were no burial goods, but the backfill contained finds dated to the late 2nd or 3rd century. Just to the south-west was a possible grave cut of a similar size and suggesting there had been another burial associated with this group.

Burial [b28] was a grave-shaped cut to the south-west of Structure 1 and containing a few badly decayed fragments of bone that did not survive lifting. The backfill of the grave contained numerous sherds of pottery and glass vessels <G6> to <G11>. One fragmented pottery vessel contained some cremated bone from an adult aged 17 to 25 years. This burial contained finds dated to the late 2nd or 3rd century, the pottery date being later than that of the glass vessels. This suggests that some level of curation may have occurred, with 'heirloom' vessels being deposited many years after their manufacture and/or acquisition. Some flakes of local tile, and two fragments of fine-grained sandstone slab, probably used for paving, were also recovered from the backfill.

There were several additional cuts within Open Area 4 (see contexts [172] and [205]) which may have been graves but did not contain any surviving human bone or other definite evidence of inhumation or cremation.

Other features within the Open Area 4 cemetery

A rectangular timber well [173] measuring 0.8m x 0.95m across and over 1.5m deep was located to the south-west of Structure 3 (see Fig 19). Only the lowest wooden planks of

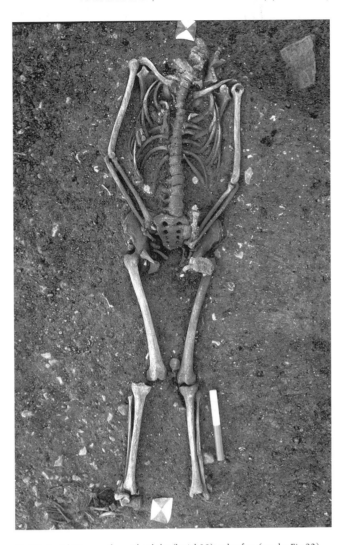

Fig 20 Burial 22, a mother with a baby (burial 23) at her foot (see also Fig 32) viewed from the north-west. The mother's skull was truncated at a later date (scale 2 x 0.10m)

the well survived as staining. The presence of wells has been noted in other cemeteries where they are thought to have been used in connection with funerary activities. The infill of the well contained finds dating to the mid 2nd century, and a quantity of brick and roof tile in early Roman fabrics, including north-west Kent and Radlett types as well as the local fabrics. Destruction flakes of north-west Kent and local tiles were present (similar to those from burials [b10] to [b12]), as well as detached tegula flanges – signs that tile reworking may have been taking place nearby. Worked oolitic limestone fragments were also recovered. None of the finds from this well was suggestive of ritual.

An empty pottery vessel [245] was found buried outside but near to the central buttress on the north-west side of the possible mausoleum structure S2, and may have once contained some form of ritual offering.

Although undated, a square pit [77] (not illustrated), some 1.20m x 1.20m square in plan, was probably Roman in date and had disturbed burial [b16]. The function of the pit is unknown.

To the north-east of the burials, in watching brief area WB1, there were two large pits containing finds dated to the 2nd century, and a possible ditch. These features were not fully excavated. A miniature pottery lamp, probably a disturbed burial good, was recovered from one of the pits. In another watching brief area, WB2, there was a small ditch or gully also dated to the 2nd century or later.

Road 1: continued use of Watling Street

Road 1 continued in use until at least the 3rd century, although the roadside ditch was apparently not kept clear (see Fig 19). A coin of Antoninus Pius (AD 138–61) was found in the fill of one section of the ditch. In another section, fragments of moulded stone including the carved stone head of a river god (see 5.3 below) were recovered. These artefacts were most likely derived from funerary structures which had been built alongside the road but had fallen into a state of disrepair. At some point, probably in the 3rd century and certainly before AD 350, a major recutting of the roadside ditch occurred and followed the same alignment as the original.

Period 3 discussion

(Table 3)
The roadside cemetery excavated at Great Dover Street appears to have been established by the mid 2nd century, and reached its most extensive development by the early 3rd century. The presence of a possible temple (B2), two walled cemeteries (S1 and S3), a possible mausoleum (S2) and contemporary burials in the surrounding area (OA4) away from the main core of the Roman settlement at Southwark, may indicate that high-status burial structures existed for some distance south-east along the line of Watling Street. Temple building B2 was apparently constructed before walled cemetery S1 and may have been the first to go out of use. The construction of mausoleum S2 may also have predated S1, although their order was less clear. Burials in the walled cemeteries were widely spaced, suggesting that they may have been private plots owned by wealthier families dwelling in the Southwark settlement.

There were only two examples of earlier burials being intercut by later burials in the open part of the cemetery, indicating that it too was well maintained. Given the lack of stratigraphic relationships between burials, the division of the burials in the open area into an early group contemporary with Building 2 and a later group contemporary with Structures 1–3 is based only on the sparse dating evidence available and should not be treated as certain. It is possible to tentatively establish the limits to the cemetery to the north-east and south-east, as no further burials were found in the surrounding watching brief areas.

Evidence for the level of decoration of the funerary structures is represented by the carved architectural stonework and by the two fragments of sculpture (for details see 5.3 below) found in the roadside ditch and in the temple (B2).

Table 3 Period 3 dating evidence (AD 120–250)

Activity	Grp	Sbgrp	Description	Date range
Building 2: a temple-mausoleum				
Fill of assoc well	8	805	BAETE 8DR20PW17; GAULI 8G; HWC; ITFEL 8; SAMLG 5DR18 <51>; VRW 7	AD 70–100
Disuse backfill of well	8	806	AHSU; FMIC 4D; HOO; HWC 2C; ITFEL 8; KOLN RCD2; SAMLG 5DR35/36, 5DR36; VRW 1C	AD 100–40
Comments: 8/806 dated on KOLN, otherwise AD 70–100.				
Structure 1: a walled cemetery				
Pit	7	702	GAULI 8G4; BBS 2F	AD 150–250
Burial 8	7	706	BAETE 8DR20PW30; BB2 2 AL, 2F OAL, 2A17, 4H, 4H WL; BBS 2, 4/5; FINE 3B BDD, 3F; GAULI 8G4; HWC 2E, 3 BDD; NKSH 2; RWS; SAMCG 6DR33; SAMLG 5, 6DR27; SAND 5A; VCWS 1B7-9; VRW	AD 140–200
Structure 3: a walled cemetery				
Burial 10	5	503	BB1 2; BB2 4H; BBS 2 AL, 2 OAL; HWC; SAMCG 4DR37; SAND 2A; VRW	AD 140–200
Burial 11	5	504	AHSU 2T; BB2 2 OAL, 2F, 4H; BBS 2F, 2 AL, 2 OAL; RWS; SAMLG 5DR18 <57>; VCWS 1; VRW	AD 140–200
Pit or grave cut	5	506	BBS 2 OAL; GAULI 8G; NKSH; RWS; SAND 2A; VRW	AD 140–200
Burial 12	5	5010	AHSU 2T; BAETE 8DR20; BBS 2 AL, 2 OAL, 5J; BHWS; GAULI 8G; NFSE 1; RWS; VCWS; VRW 9A	AD 140–200
Open Area 4: burials and features outside B2 and S1–3				
Fill of timber-lined well	9	401	BAETE 8DR20; BB2 4H AL; BBS 2 OAL; GAULI 8G; HWC 2T; LOMA 6; NFSE 7; NKSH 2; RWS; SAMCG 4DR37; SAMMV 4DR37; VRW 7HOF, 1H	AD 140–60
Burial 17	9	907	BB2 4H; NVCC 1DX; SAMMV; SAND 2A; VRW	AD 150–250
Burial 15	9	9016	AHBB 4H; BBS 2 OAL, 2F; GAULI 8G; HWB; VRW	AD 140–250
Bustum burial 1	9	9019	AHSU 2; BAETE 8DR20; CGWH 9LA; FMIC; VRW 2C, 9C	AD 50–130
External deposit	9	9027	AHSU; BB1 2F; BBS 2 AL; CADIZ; GAULI 8G; HWC 2E, 3F; LOXI 5J; RHOD3 8C184; RWS; SAMLG 4DR30; VRW	AD 120–60
Burial 28 cremation	9	9037	BB2 2 OAL, 2F, 5J WL; BB2F 4/5; BBS 2 OAL, 2F, 4/5; BHWS; CCIMP 3J; GAULI; LOXI 9A; MOSL 3; RWS; SAND 4H; VCWS 2T; VRW 2K, 2T	AD 200–50

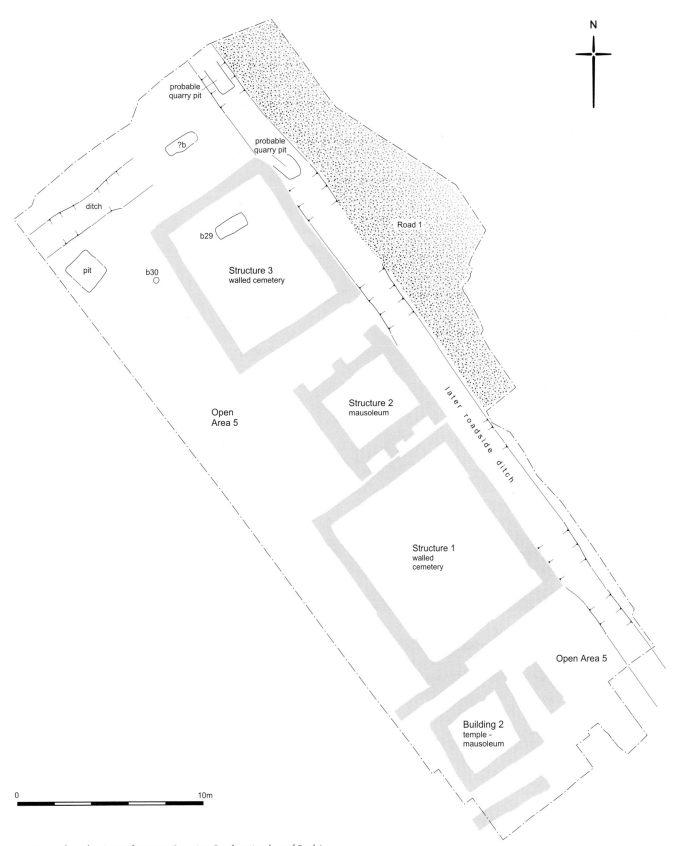

N

Fig 21 Period 4 – late Roman features in Open Area 5 and continued use of Road 1

The sculpture included the bearded head of a deity (see Fig 41), likely to have been either Dionysiac, or representing a water deity such as Oceanus, Neptune or even Tamesis. Either subject would have been appropriate to a funerary context. The other architectural piece, a pine cone, is the first example from the south of the Roman province; other examples in Britain have so far been confined to military sites in northern England, Wales and Scotland. The pine cone may have decorated the funeral monument of one of the military personnel present in either the Roman settlement on the site of Southwark or of the City of London.

2.4 Period 4: the late Roman cemetery (AD 250–400)

(Table 4)

Use of the roadside cemetery continued into the late Roman period and included some burials (Fig 21). In walled cemetery structure S3 there was one further inhumation burial and a late cremation burial was located in the external area to its west (OA5). To the south, cemetery structures S1 and S2 had apparently fallen out of use by this time. Road 1 continued in use into the 4th century.

Structure 1: walled cemetery

Walled cemetery S1 apparently went out of use in the 3rd century, with the internal structures falling into disrepair. Parts of the outer wall may also have been robbed at that time.

Structure 2: mausoleum

There is no evidence to suggest that the mausoleum was still in use in Period 4.

Structure 3: walled cemetery

One further burial [b29] (see Fig 21; see Fig 36 for detail) appears to have taken place within the enclosed area of walled cemetery S3. A child aged 6 to 12 years had been laid extended supine with the head to the north-east. Evidence for a wooden coffin was found. The skeleton had been heavily disturbed by an undated pit [121] which may have been associated with Open Area 5. The burial contained finds dated to the mid 3rd century and it is possible that the robbing of the outer wall of the enclosure also took place during this period.

Open Area 5: unenclosed cemetery area

In the open area to the north and west of the walled cemetery S3, there was further burial activity (see Fig 21). A pottery vessel contained the cremation burial [b30] of a male aged over 45 years. The vessel, buried upright, bore graffito on the outside, and the cremation dated to the mid 3rd century or later. A cut [142], which contained some disarticulated human bone and iron nails, may have been part of another burial and had been disturbed at its north-west end by a small circular pit [85] that contained rubble and is of unknown function. To the north-west a ditch [93] ran south-east to north-west and disturbed burials [b3] and [b13]. The ditch may have been for drainage but its north-eastern extent was truncated by post-medieval activity. It had silted up and was subsequently redug as a smaller gully [91] on a slightly different alignment. A square rubbish pit [45] lay nearby but may be considered as part of Open Area 6 activities.

Road 1: continued use of Watling Street

Road 1 continued in use in the mid 3rd to 4th centuries. The roadside ditch had become infilled with silt and the whole length was redug. To the north-west and on the line of the roadside ditch two deeper cuts, probably quarry pits, suggested that extraction of natural gravel took place, perhaps to repair the road surface (Fig 22). The ditch subsequently silted up, the fills containing a large amount of pottery dated c AD 350–400. At Arcadia Buildings the road apparently went out of use in the late 3rd century, with the road surface even being quarried, but was reinstated in the 4th century.

The large amount of pottery recovered from the infill of the late Roman ditch at Great Dover Street adds to the corpus of late Roman pottery in London and to discussion of the later settlement in Roman Southwark (see 5.1 below). Building material from the late ditch included fragments of possible wall render in *opus signinum* mortar, a slab of Purbeck marble and one small hard chalk tessera, probably from a good-quality floor mosaic. Ceramic building material included a wider range of tile types than had been recovered from earlier periods, and included tile in late local fabric (c AD 140–250) and a number of flue tile fragments. The pottery and the wide range of tile fabrics and forms suggest that the material did not originate on the site of the cemetery.

Table 4 Period 4 dating evidence (AD 250–400)

Activity	Grp	Sbgrp	Description	Date range
Road 1 and Open Area 5				
Rdside ditch	10	308	AHFA 3 END; BAET 8DR20; BAETE 8DR20; BB1; OXRC	AD 270–400
Rdside ditch	10	1002	AHFA; BBS 2 OL; NVCC; OXRC 4, 4 STD; OXWC 7WC7; PORD; RWS; VRW 2T	AD 350–400
Rdside ditch	10	1004	AHFA 2FX, 2V, 4M; BAETL 8DR20; BB1 5J ARCS; NVCC 4/5; OXRC 4 ROD, 7C100, 7C98 WPD; PORD 2	AD 350–400
Burial 29 in OA5	13	508	AHFA; AHSU 2T; BAETE 8; BB2 4H; BBS 2F; FMIC 3; NVCC 3 NCD, 3K END; SAMCG 3DE72; SAMLG 4RT12; TSK 2T	AD 250–300
Robbing of S1	13	7010	AHFA 2AX, 2 COMB; BB1 4G226, 4M; BBS 4H; COLWW 7; HWB; NKSH 2; OXRC 4; SAMLG 4, 5DR18, 5DR36; VRR	AD 270–400
Small ditch	13	9024	AHFA 2; BAETE 8; BB1 5J ARCS; BB2 4H; BBS 2F; CADIZ 8; GAUL1 8; NVCC 2; SAMEG; VRW 7HOF	AD 250–400

Comments: 10/308 dated on AHFA indented beaker to AD 225–400 (Millett 1979, 134) but fabric queried; 10/1002 and 10/1004 dated on PORD; 13/508 NVCC 3K dated from mid 2nd century onwards.

2.5 Period 5: post-Roman activity (AD 400+)

Open Area 6 and other post-Roman activity

The latest extant Roman activity recorded in some areas of the site was sealed by dark earth deposits, which due to time constraints were removed by machine. Other post-Roman activity included a late medieval rubbish pit [34] dated 1350–1500, and numerous other pits from the 17th to 19th century in date. Some of the pits contained large amounts of domestic rubbish, and one also contained a pipeclay figurine of a king, possibly James I. Roman hobnails and a pottery lamp recovered from the pits are likely to have been dispersed burial goods. Several brick wells or soakaways, a brick cellar and brick walls from the 19th century were the most recent features recorded.

Fig 22 The late Roman roadside ditch with a quarry pit cut into its base, viewed from the south-east (scale 5 x 0.10m)

3

Aspects of the Roman roadside cemetery

3.1 The cemetery population

Bill White

The 25 inhumation and five cremation burials from the Great Dover Street site provide an insight into burial customs. The inhumation skeletons, in particular, provide some information on demography, family grouping and pathology in this part of Southwark during the 2nd and 3rd centuries AD. Up to 12 of the individuals (including both sexes and all ages) and possibly two more were buried in wooden coffins. The evidence is confined to soil staining and the survival of a few nails; no other coffin fittings survived. Three of the inhumation burials, [b25], [b26] and [b27], were packed with chalk. Two other burials involved the use of chalk: [b17] was laid on a bed of chalk and [b7] had some chalk in the grave fill. Burial [b14] was laid on a bed of gravel within a possible masonry structure. At least one-third of the burials were accompanied by burial goods. The bodies were buried supine and extended except for two prone burials (8.3%), a higher proportion than in the eastern cemetery (2.5%) (Barber & Bowsher 2000). There was a single burial, [b8], showing (post-mortem) decapitation where the cranium had been placed in an unusual position – on the chest – rather than between the legs (Harman *et al* 1981). The practice of leaving the lower jaw in its original position was also noted in two individuals in the eastern cemetery (Barber & Bowsher 2000).

The inhumation burials included a high proportion of children, eight of them (33.3%) having died under the age of 13. Furthermore, about two-thirds of the disarticulated skeletons were immature. A further two burials (8.3%) were of adolescents (aged 13 to 16). This compares with children representing 14.1% of the sample at the eastern cemetery of Roman London (Conheeney 2000), 20.0% at St Bartholomew's, London (Bentley & Pritchard 1982), 17.4% at Cirencester (McWhirr *et al* 1982) and 23.9% at Lankhills, Winchester (Clarke 1979). The high proportion of children may be linked to family groupings (see below).

Half of the adults could not be assigned to a specific age range but four had died very young (17 to 25 years old). Three lived possibly into their forties but none could be shown to have exceeded the age of 45. Among the cremation burials one man [b30] had died over the age of 45. Five of the adult inhumation burials were male (20.8%), six (25.0%) were female, the remaining five (20.8%) being insufficiently complete to be sexed. Among the five cremation burials two were identified as male and one was female. The Great Dover Street site is remarkable then in showing no excess of males over females in the cemetery and is therefore comparable to Poundbury (Waldron 1994) and Ancaster (Cox 1989).

It was not possible to calculate an average height since too few long bones remained intact. However, in the four examples quoted here the men were significantly taller than the women, as has been found in Romano-British sites in London and elsewhere (J Conheeney, pers comm). The same four individuals provided data used to calculate the limb-bone shaft indices. The mean metric index for the two females was 89.0 and that for males 82.9. The cnemic index was 78.4 for two females and only the index calculated for one of the males, 64.9, was suggestive of unusual flattening of the shaft.

None of the skulls was sufficiently intact for craniometry. Non-metric traits of the cranium were noted but were found to be rare: lambdoid wormian bones were found in three burials (one of whom was immature), that is, 21.4% of possible cases, there was a child with a retained metopic suture (7.1% of possible cases) and one adult individual had both lower third molars congenitally absent (16.7% of possible cases). Post-cranial traits likewise were rare. One woman had bilateral septal apertures of the humerus (14.3% of possible cases). There was a single occurrence of spondylolysis of the fifth lumbar vertebra (16.7% of possible cases) and one of sacralisation of the fifth lumbar vertebra (16.7% of possible cases). Combinations of such traits were not observed and so could not be used to confirm family clusterings of burials.

Some form of dental hygiene may have been practised since the accumulation of dental calculus was confined to one male and conformed to the finding at the eastern cemetery that women practised better dental hygiene than men (Conheeney 2000). Dental caries were rare (7.2%), affecting molars only and interproximally. Periodontalism was rare and mild (two cases).

There was some evidence of dietary deficiency at the site. The skull of one of the children, [b11], showed parietal osteoporosis, possibly a manifestation of iron-deficiency anaemia. However, there was no trace of cribra orbitalia, its more common manifestation. One child, [b26], had its limbs affected by rickets suggesting that it had either experienced a diet lacking in vitamin D or was sickly and unable to absorb it. However, the majority of the children (87.5%) showed no sign of rickets, although other Romano-British sites have produced evidence of the disease (Conheeney 2000).

By contrast, a man [b18] and a woman [b27] showed possible evidence of dietary excess. In each case osteophytes were forming on the right side of the bodies of thoracic vertebrae, beginning the calcification of the longitudinal ligament of the spine. This was considered to be the incipient form of 'DISH' (Diffuse Idiopathic Skeletal Hyperostosis), a disease that today affects chiefly obese men over the age of 50 who are enjoying a rich diet but a sedentary life (Resnick & Niwayama 1988).

Osteoarthritis was the only common disease. The parts of the skeleton affected were the spine (11.1% of possible cases), the elbow (17.6% of possible cases), the wrist (10.0% of possible cases) and the ankle joints (21.4% of possible cases).

One young man, [b25], had sustained a compound fracture of the left lower leg, which had healed badly causing a shortening of the limb. A total of three broken ribs was found, and two tibiae showed periostitis following trauma (18.2% of possible cases).

The population as a whole appear rather short-lived by comparison with other Romano-British groups. They seem not to have suffered serious illnesses or injuries but this may be a concomitant of the short lifespan. Standards of dental hygiene were high.

Unfortunately, non-metric variation was not sufficiently explicit for family groupings to be confirmed via skeletal characteristics. However, such groupings may possibly be inferred from the clusters of burials with a high proportion of these being immature persons, as in the small cemetery identified at St Bartholomew's Hospital, London (Bentley & Pritchard 1982) and at Lankhills, Winchester (Clarke 1979). This may be particularly true of the cluster of burials [b10], [b11], [b12] and [b29] around the mortared plinth in the walled cemetery (Structure 3) which consisted of a woman and three children, although [b29] was apparently later in date. The three chalk burials, [b25], [b26] and [b27], may also be a family group. The burial of a newborn child at a woman's feet, [b22] and [b23], is highly suggestive of a mother and her baby.

3.2 Funerary rites, burial practice and belief

Angela Wardle

Although the burials from Great Dover Street form a relatively small group, there is evidence for a variety of burial rites and some tenuous evidence for funerary belief. The discussion considers evidence from the graves themselves and the objects placed in them and artefacts found in non-burial contexts, which are considered to be displaced or residual burial goods.

Cremation burials

Cremation burial was more prevalent in the first two centuries AD, but its popularity later declined, although there are many instances of its survival into the 4th century (Barber & Bowsher 2000). In this part of the southern cemetery three cremation burials were placed in ceramic vessels [52], [89] and [48], the latter dating to the 3rd or 4th century. There is evidence among the residual glassware for glass cinerary urns, as have been found elsewhere in London (eg MoL A14398 from Bishopsgate: Wheeler 1930, 42, pl xiv, 1; RCHME 1928, fig 65, 32). The site has also produced the first example of a square jar used as a cinerary urn in London.

When studying the artefacts associated with cremation burials it is important to make a distinction between those placed on the bier and burned with the body as part of the ceremony and those deposited as offerings with the cremated remains. Despite careful examination, the residues from four of the five cremation burials from Great Dover Street produced no burnt artefacts. The cremation burial in the *bustum* and identified as that of a female, produced an important collection of unburnt burial goods (lamps and tazze), described in detail in the catalogue below. There were also fragments of molten glass present, probably representing burnt glass vessels.

The choice of lamps appears to be deliberate as Anubis, the Egyptian god of judgement who controlled entry to the underworld, is a particularly apt subject for a burial. The jackal-headed god was a nephew of the goddess Isis and became her guardian and guide, assisting in her search for the dead Osiris (Serapis). A lamp in the British Museum (Inv no. D 285, BM 279) shows Isis standing between Harpocrates and Anubis (Tran Tam Tinh 1972, pl XXII, figs 27, 28; Bailey 1988). A figure with the jackal's head of Anubis leads an Isiac procession on a lamp from France (Vertet 1969, 125, fig 16a). In Graeco-Roman mythology Anubis was equated with the god Hermes/Mercury, the conductor of souls (Psychopompus), and the Greek name Hermanubis reflected this assimilation. In the tradition handed down by Plutarch (Isis and Osiris 12–20) Anubis also symbolised victory of life over death, leading the dead to their resurrection. Witt (1971, 208) suggests that to anyone professing the Isiac faith, Anubis/Mercury was as familiar a figure as an undertaker in Christian communities, and priests are known to have enacted the role of Anubis in funeral rites, suitably clad in a jackal's head mask (Witt 1971, fig 46). The cult of Isis which spread throughout the Roman Empire was of particular appeal to women (Heyob 1975; Turcan 1996, 95–104). There is well-known evidence for the presence of an Iseum, or temple of the cult, in London, where a pottery flagon said to be from Tooley Street, Southwark bears an inscription referring to a temple (Harris & Harris 1965, 79–80) and an inscription records the restoration of a temple (Hassall in Hill et al 1980, 195). Objects which suggest the presence of members of the cult in London have also been recognised, most recently the reattribution of a bone hairpin from Moorgate Street as Isis (Johns 1996; Henig 1984, 113). It is possible that in this burial we have further indirect evidence, certainly for the rites of an eastern cult, perhaps that of Isis.

The presence of the fallen gladiator lamp adds a further dimension to the picture, and it might be significant that in the arena slaves dressed as Mercury Psychopompus or Charon dragged away the fallen bodies (Grant 1967, 76). The cremated remains are those of a woman and one should consider the possibility that she was a gladiator, a practice which may have been more common than is generally realised (N Bateman, pers comm). Literary sources refer to the existence of female gladiators from the time of Nero onwards (Balsdon 1969, 291). Although most references are pejorative, decrying the excesses of Nero and Domitian (Tacitus, Annals 15.32; Suetonius, Domitian 4.1) and satirising the scandals of Roman life (Juvenal, Satires 6.246–7), the fact that Septimius Severus found it necessary to forbid the practice at the end of the 2nd century implies that it was sufficiently widespread to incur censure (Cassius Dio (Sept Sev) 75.16.1). Epigraphical and iconographic evidence noted by Wiedemann (1992) includes a relief from the eastern Mediterranean in the British Museum showing women engaged in combat. Clearly an interpretation of the cremation burial as that of a female

gladiator can only be speculative and may indeed be too simplistic, but it is certainly possible. An alternative, and perhaps more acceptable interpretation, is that the lamp symbolises funeral games, the origin of gladiatorial combat in Republican times.

The lamps show no obvious sign of use as they were not sooted. Similar conclusions have been made about lamps at other sites which are reported to have been unused or which show only a little sooting (Down & Rule 1971, 71). The breakages appear to be post-burial damage rather than deliberate destruction as only two were badly damaged. Whether or not the body was cremated in the pit, the lamps and tazze were placed in the fill after the pyre had been extinguished. There is no obvious pattern to the deposition of the ceramic objects, the positions of which appear to be haphazard. It appears the cremation residue was scattered throughout the deposit but a concentration was noted under one of the tazza. Several of the tazze were inverted; two had been placed over lamps and three of the remaining lamps were very close to single vessels or groups of tazze (see Fig 24).

The occurrence of tazze within burials frequently accompanied by lamps is well documented (Philpott 1991, 193). However, the high number of tazze in the pit is unusual. The state of the vessels suggests they may have been used once prior to burial, possibly as part of the cremation or interment ritual, and then carefully placed with the lamps into the pit. Multiple offerings of lamps, beakers, dishes and tazze were found at Mucking in a burial dating to the late 2nd century, these lying in a charcoal deposit which also contained pine seeds (Pinus pinea) (Philpott 1991, 193). Don Bailey (pers comm) reported that the objects were thrown into the pit in no particular order and several of the lamps, which are all degenerate versions of Loeschcke Type IXb, were made from the same mould and were of British manufacture. At Baldock, a circular pit contained 31 wheelmade lamps and 15 pedestal cups, placed over the cremated remains of a juvenile (Stead & Rigby 1986, 78–81). Although the cups were similar in design to tazze they had hollow stems and it was suggested could have functioned as candlesticks. Additionally these vessels had not been carefully placed in the pit but were thought to represent debris from a ritual which may have involved the smashing of vessels. Multiple offerings of lamps, sometimes with tazze, are also found, for example at Colchester (Philpott 1991, 191), one of the earliest sites where lamps, a Roman introduction to Britain, occur.

Three more lamps were found at Great Dover Street. Two are small plain 'factory' lamps (Firmalampen) in local fabrics, rather poorly moulded and perhaps made for the funeral trade. Neither was associated with a burial, but were almost certainly displaced burial goods, one from a ditch, the other from a pit. The third was incomplete and came from a post-medieval pit. Lamps fulfilled both practical and symbolic functions, providing light for the dead on their journey to the underworld, giving light for the dead in their new surroundings, and as familiar domestic objects serving as a link between the living and the dead (Alcock 1980, 61).

It is extremely likely that the antler amulet (<112> [53]) found in a roadside ditch also came originally from a grave. The discovery of an antler pendant in a cemetery is entirely appropriate. Greep (1994, 82) points out that antler was believed to possess prophylactic powers, quoting Pliny (*Natural history* 8.49.112–19) who notes that the right horn of a stag has healing properties. Antler pendants were frequently carved with a phallus, a powerful symbol used as a good luck charm and for protection, and although the pendant from Great Dover Street is undecorated, it is probable that the antler itself was considered protective. The shedding and renewal of the antler could itself be symbolic of rebirth (Greep 1994, 83). The pendant is complete and unburnt, and similar to continental examples may have been placed in a grave.

Inhumation burials

Twelve, and possibly up to 14, of the 25 inhumation burials on site were in wooden coffins. Evidence was limited to iron nails. One body [b14] was laid within a stone and possibly tile cist; this may also have had a coffin but the evidence was ambiguous. The most noticeable special rite involved the use of chalk. Three bodies were packed with chalk, burials [b25 to b27], a fourth was laid on a bed of chalk, [b17], and another had some chalk within the fill, [b7]. The location of these burials within the walled cemetery implies either respect being paid to a central high-status individual or that the entire group were of high status.

Burial goods

Eleven (36%) of the burials were accompanied by burial goods. It is presumed that ceramic and glass vessels and their contents placed in graves provided sustenance or other necessities in the afterlife. A total of 26 pottery vessels were associated with either inhumation or cremation burials from Great Dover Street: 7 were from inhumation burials, 3 others contained cremation burials. There were also 8 tazze from the *bustum* and a further 8 shattered vessels from the very disturbed burial [b28]. In addition there were the tettina, the 'votive' jar and the near complete Gauloise amphora.

The vessels from burials comprise 3 jars, 3 flagons and 1 beaker. None of the types has an exceptional fabric or form, only two are in a fine ware (Nene Valley Colour-coated ware), which is a common fabric especially in the 3rd century. As the sample of vessels from burials is so small, it is difficult to define any trends within the choice of forms selected. Most of the vessels were complete albeit broken and the edges of the sherds indicated that they had been broken at or shortly after burial. The evidence from the vessels from the cremation burials especially the tazze suggests that they were not broken deliberately. The evidence from the inhumation burials is more difficult to assess: some of the burials had been disturbed. Burial [b8] was the most obvious with the skull having been placed on the chest. Vessels could easily have been broken

especially if those opening the grave were not aware of the existence or position of them. Evidence from the eastern cemetery suggests that the deliberate smashing of vessels is not a common ritual (Barber & Bowsher 2000, 124–5): only three out of a total of 200 vessels were thought to have been broken in this way.

Vessels found in burials can have been reused. Previous excavations at Great Dover Street revealed a Black-burnished ware everted-rim jar which was soot encrusted and thought to have been used for some time prior to burial (Graham 1978, 479, fig 220, no. 1870). However, due to the level of abrasion especially on the surfaces of the vessels it has not been possible to say whether the pots from this excavation were used or unused. The exception is the Alice Holt storage jar associated with cremation burial [b30] where the graffiti suggests a former use for the vessel.

The similarity in form and surface appearance of one of the jars in [b8] to the fabric of Thameside Kent Black-burnished-type ware is discussed in the burial catalogue below. In addition, similarities to this fabric were also noted in regard to jars from [b28] and the 'votive' jar [245]. Everted-rim jars in this fabric are the most common jar form from the eastern cemetery and are generally dated c AD 180–300 in London. None of the Great Dover Street jars matches the fabric description of this ware. However, as most of the vessels were complete from the eastern cemetery, only one example of this fabric has been analysed and there may be wider variability within the fabric. Therefore it is not possible at this time to clarify the source of these jars from Great Dover Street.

Some of the more well-known burial rites, such as the provision of a coin to pay Charon's fee, are not seen at Great Dover Street, although there are only a few instances of this practice in the London cemeteries (Hall 1996; Barber & Bowsher 2000). Apart from one brooch from a grave fill [b21] there are no items of jewellery, dress accessories or other personal ornament found in direct association with any burial. Moreover, it is unlikely that this brooch was originally from [b21], which is disturbed and the skeleton incomplete. The date of the brooch, which is also incomplete, is considerably earlier than the date of the pottery in the grave fill. A second complete brooch from Structure 1 is likely to have been a burial good, perhaps originally worn, but cannot now be associated with any specific burial. Similarly a small bracelet, suitable for a child, is typical of the jewellery found in Roman burials, either worn or deposited by the body.

One fragment of jet pin was discovered in [b26], although this too could have been redeposited. Jet was a fashionable material for hairpins during the later Roman period. It is known that it was worked in northern Britain, with the most well-known centre at York, close to the main sources of the raw material (Allason-Jones 1996, 1–7). Most finds of jet jewellery have been from graves and the material, prized for its electrostatic properties, was thought to ward off evil and have beneficial effects.

Shoes are thought to have been placed in graves to ensure that the deceased was adequately shod for the journey to the underworld. Four burials contained hobnails, the only surviving remains of leather footwear, and there is another shoe among the residual finds. In some cases, for example [b26], the only evidence was staining of the soil, and in others the existence of shoes only became apparent after examination of the X-rays of the accessioned iron fragments. Iron objects on the site were generally poorly preserved perhaps due to a fluctuating moisture content of the soil. In no case was it possible to reconstruct the nail pattern or determine the type of shoe. The gender and age profile varied from that of the eastern cemetery in that two of the four burials provided with shoes are of adult females, one (unsexed) child is aged between 6 and 12, and there is only one adult male. In the eastern cemetery (Barber & Bowsher 2000, 137–8) it was more common to find footwear in male graves, but this is perhaps a reflection of the types of shoe worn by women and children, which could be constructed without nails, rather than differential treatment of the sexes. There is no evidence that any of the shoes from these burials had actually been worn by the corpse. Two were found at the foot of the grave, a very common position, but one, from [b22], appears to have been placed on the body, over the left side of the pelvis. In [b16] the hobnails were recovered from the area of the torso, later activity having removed both the head and feet of the burial.

Other artefacts were sometimes provided to sustain the deceased and to provide entertainment in the afterlife. The only article of this type was a glass gaming counter. This was not necessarily a burial good as such artefacts are commonly found in ordinary domestic contexts, but gaming sets have been found in graves, for example Lullingstone (Meates 1979) and London (Barber & Bowsher 2000, 135–6).

3.3 Architectural evidence for the structures

External appearance

The tile-working horizon found in the area of walled cemetery S3 shows there was at least one tile-roofed building in the area. This may have been the possible temple, Building 2, as this was out of use by the time the other structures were built. As well as roofing, tiles could have been used for decorative effects on the facades (both external and on internal walls and monuments). Two fragments of unusual, knife-trimmed imbrices were found in the later roadside ditch. Although damaged, it is possible that these may have had a decorative crest, though there is no firm evidence of this.

A cut block of calcareous tufa from the timber well in Open Area 4 is likely to have been used as part of a vaulted ceiling in one of the structures, possibly the mausoleum (S2). It is possible that S2 also had a tiled roof in addition to an arched vault.

Material which may have been used to face the walls of the structures includes Kentish ragstone and flints; a group of eight roughly knapped flint nodules was noted from a post-medieval pit. Walled cemetery S3 would have looked different to the structures as the outer walls appear to have been constructed of mortared flint rubble rather than the Kentish ragstone that predominated in the others.

There is no structural evidence for window openings in any of the buildings, but one piece of natural green-blue window glass <G23> was recovered from the backfill of the central robbed feature in S1.

The most compelling evidence for the external appearance is that from the sculpted stone fragments. These comprised the head of a possible water deity, a carved pine-cone finial and two fragments of stone cornice moulding. They are described in detail in section 5.3. All the items are likely to have derived from the excavated structures. It is likely the head of the bearded deity <A1> architectural fragment formed part of a group of sculpture associated with one of the funerary monuments, rather than being associated with any temple structure.

The pine-cone finial is funerary, but its context, in the packing of the cut for an amphora burial in the walled cemetery S1, indicates that the monument to which it had belonged had already fallen into disrepair. The larger of the two plain mouldings, <A3>, was found in the same context and may thus have formed part of the same monument. The other plain moulding, <A4>, probably belonged to another monument, since it is of different stone and proportions from <A3>. Fig 23 is a reconstruction of how the site may have looked in the mid 2nd century.

Internal appearance

The best evidence for the internal finish of these structures, or at least one of them, is provided by the fragments of *opus signinum* wall plaster/render painted with red ochre which occur in association with Structure 3, and Open Areas 2 and 4. As none was found in the robber trench of the outer wall of S3, it would appear that *opus signinum* was possibly used as wall render on the central feature there. All the plaster had a similar finish, the colour having been applied directly to the smoothed *opus signinum* surface rather than to a layer of white plaster, or *intonaco*, as is usual in domestic or bath-house environments. The flake of Reigate stone adhered to one fragment and a brick with red-painted *opus signinum* attached both show that this finish was applied to a structure or structures. All the fragments of red-painted plaster were plain. Parallels for the use of painted plaster in cemeteries can be found in the mausolea at Poundbury, Dorset (Farwell & Molleson 1993).

The only evidence for the use of veneers or paving comes from the slab of Purbeck marble, 33mm thick, from the 4th-century infill of the roadside ditch. This stone slab, though rather decayed, had at least one sawn face. One abraded 15mm thick slab of fine-grained sandstone from [b28] had mortar on the sides and base, and had probably been used as flooring.

Fig 23 *A reconstruction of the Period 3 mid 2nd-century funerary structures along the south-west side of Road 1 as viewed from the east (by Kikar Singh)*

A single small tessera in white chalk, of the type used in mosaics, was recorded from Open Area 5. However, much of the other associated material from this period seems to differ in character so it may have been brought from elsewhere.

3.4 The cemetery in its wider context

With no known fixed boundary to Roman Southwark the extent of the southern cemetery area is poorly defined. There are two distinct cemetery areas. The majority of burials are found to the south of the junction of Stane Street and Watling Street and alongside them. Some of these burials apparently occur some distance from the main settlement. The second group are found along a road that is thought to link the Southwark bridgehead with Lambeth. There is also evidence of later Roman burials (Cowan 1992) that take place inside the settled area after the contraction of the urban settlement.

There is antiquarian evidence for Roman burials in the area of the site, particularly in Tabard Street (Hall 1996). The Great Dover Street excavation produced the largest number of Roman burials (25 inhumation and five cremation burials) to have been discovered on one site in Southwark. With

two walled cemeteries, a mausoleum, a possible temple-mausoleum, and sculpted and worked stone fragments the site is an important addition to the study of Roman London. Until this site investigation, excavated evidence for high-status funerary structures was limited in London, although it should be noted that the masonry 'signal tower' excavated at Shadwell in 1975 has now been reinterpreted as a possible tower mausoleum (Lakin in prep). Recent excavations at Spitalfields have also found further evidence for mausoleum structures (Chris Thomas, pers comm).

Roman walled cemeteries are well documented from the south-east (Black 1986) with examples such as Langley and Springhead containing masonry structures such as tombs and towers. More rare is the temple-mausoleum type of building. Examples at Lullingstone (Meates 1979) and Bancroft (Williams & Zeepvat 1994) had sarcophagi in subterranean cuts. Excavated moulded and carved stone are rare in the London region; in Southwark apart from the spectacular finds beneath Southwark Cathedral (Hammerson 1978) there are only a few fragments known to be from funerary contexts. Here the moulded cornices, pine cone and the head of the god or river deity must have come from either the mausoleum or other structures located within these walled cemeteries.

The use of Reigate stone (in B2, S2 and in at least one

base in S1) is not very common in the Roman period, although recently it has been noted in pre-Boudican buildings along Borough High Street (Drummond-Murray & Thompson in prep). The occurrence of disarticulated horse bones is an aspect of cemetery activity that has been noted before (Rielly 2000). The site also had a *bustum* which contained charred plant remains and a large number of ceramic lamps and tazze. Three of the lamps carried images of the Egyptian god Anubis and another that of a fallen gladiator.

When the roadside ditch was redug in the late 3rd century some of the funeral structures were in a state of disrepair. This shows that the road was still in use or had been re-established as was found at Arcadia Buildings. This ditch silted up in the late 4th century and was found to contain a large amount of domestic pottery that showed Roman Southwark was still thriving.

The location of the burials may be a function of the changing size of the population; certainly a building was dismantled and several ditches were infilled before the main cemetery was begun. However, the location alongside a

major road into the settlement and the presence of funerary structures imply either a high-status or wealthy burial population (Niblett 1999). The high percentage of burial goods and the various funerary structures suggest wealth may be a factor. The Great Dover Street population shows a more even spread of the sexes than usually seen in excavated Romano-British cemeteries. How unusual this is can only be answered by further excavation and study of Roman Southwark's southern cemetery.

In conclusion, the excavation has produced important results. It demonstrates that burials, substantial masonry funerary structures and a possible temple existed in Southwark along the line of at least one Roman road, remarkably more than 400m from St George's Church which currently is thought to lie in the vicinity of the southern extent of the Roman settlement in Southwark (Harvey Sheldon, pers comm). This in turn suggests that the archaeological potential of this area of Southwark may be much greater than was previously appreciated, and that Roman roadside cemeteries may have extended for a considerable distance away from the urban core.

4

Catalogue of burials and associated finds

This chapter presents more detailed descriptions of the osteological and artefactual character of each burial, arranged chronologically and with the artefacts divided by type. A catalogue of burials is given in Table 5, and a summary of the cremated human remains in Table 6. Additional information about the human bone can be found in section 5.4, and in Tables 16 and 17 which summarise characteristics of selected inhumation burials.

4.1 The burials and associated finds

Burial 1

(Figs 24–6)
Cremation burial in pit or *bustum*
Adult; female. Weight 1.0kg
1st/2nd century

Lamps

<P1> <20> [38] (Fig 25)
Volute lamp; Loeschcke Type IV. L 97; w 67; h 24.5mm
Complete. The discus shows a fallen gladiator, a Samnite, wearing a crested helmet, sword in right hand, his left arm raised to his face, with his shield in front of him. Loeschcke shoulder form VIb (Bailey 1988, ix). The filling hole is off-centre, between the figure's head and his shield and there is a small air hole in the nozzle channel, which shows possible traces of sooting (?slip). Fabric Central Gaulish White ware (CGWH), patchy light brown to black slip, very abraded on the discus.

There is an identical (but blurred) version of this form in the British Museum collection, found at Poultry (Bailey 1988, vii III, 161, Q1530) and another also from Lombard Street, MoL 1425 (Central Gaulish fabric). The type is also well known on the Continent, for example from Vindonissa, where it dates from the late 1st/2nd century (Leibundgut 1977, nos 445–8, table 1; 220, table 42) and Trier (Goethert-Polaschek 1985, nos 488, 535, table 54).

<P2> <23> [38] (Fig 25)
Volute lamp; Loeschcke Type IV. L 101; w 71; h 24–29mm
Complete. The discus shows Anubis. The figure, facing left, has what appears to be a jackal's head, somewhat blurred, on which its identification as Anubis is based. It wears a short tunic, and the right arm is raised; a wand or sceptre, the herald's caduceus, which identifies the god with Mercury, is held in the left hand. The filling hole is placed to the left of the figure, as in the following examples also. No traces of sooting. The body of the lamp is distorted and it has an irregular incised foot-ring. It was probably damaged in the kiln and is now lopsided. Fabric Central Gaulish White ware (CGWH), patchy dark grey brown slip.

The figure type appears to be rare, certainly in Britain.

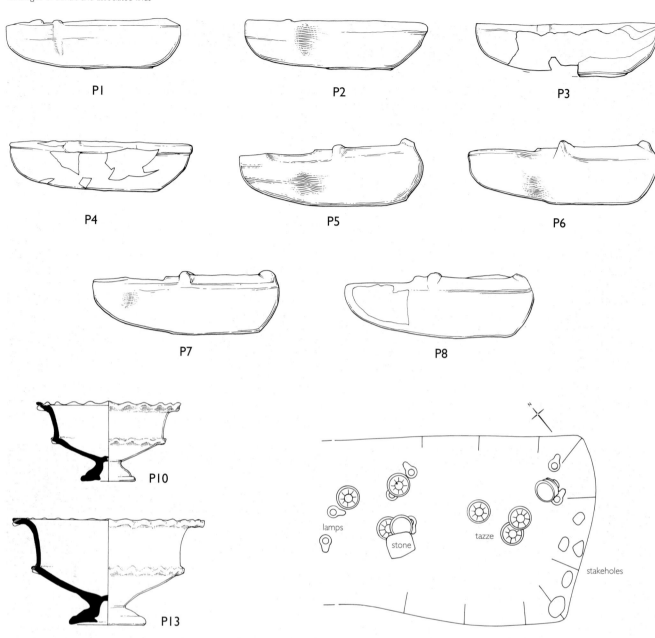

Fig 24 Plan of burial 1, a bustum, showing stakeholes along the base of its south-eastern side which may have supported a pyre above the cut (scale 1:20). Two of the tazze <P10> and <P13> (scale 1:4) and the eight pottery lamps <P1> – <P8> (scale 1:2) recovered from the fill of the bustum

Vertet (1969, 125, fig 16b) publishes an incomplete example from Caerleon, thought to be made in Lyon, on which the figure is in identical pose, with a context date of the Caerleon lamp of AD 75–140. Another from a burial at Chichester is apparently in the same Gaulish fabric as those from Great Dover Street (Down & Rule 1971, 99, burial 74, fig 5.22).

<P3> <4><6> [38] (Fig 25)
Volute lamp; Loeschcke Type IV. L 100mm; h 29mm
Incomplete. The discus shows the Egyptian deity Anubis. The jackal's head, with long ears, upraised right hand and wand or caduceus in left are well moulded. About three-quarters of the lamp is present, with much of the base and side wall missing, but it was smashed and sufficiently scattered in the

pit for it to be accessioned as two separate objects originally. There are no traces of sooting. Fabric Central Gaulish White ware (CGWH), patchy orange brown slip.

<P4> <30> [38] (Fig 25)
Volute lamp; Loeschcke Type IV. L 101mm
Almost complete. This discus shows Anubis in a similar pose, but the details, for example of the legs, suggest that this is from a different mould from <4>, even allowing for the continuing reuse of a mould. The lamp was broken in the pit but is substantially complete, with part of the side wall and a little of the discus missing. Fabric Central Gaulish White ware (CGWH), patchy dark brown slip.

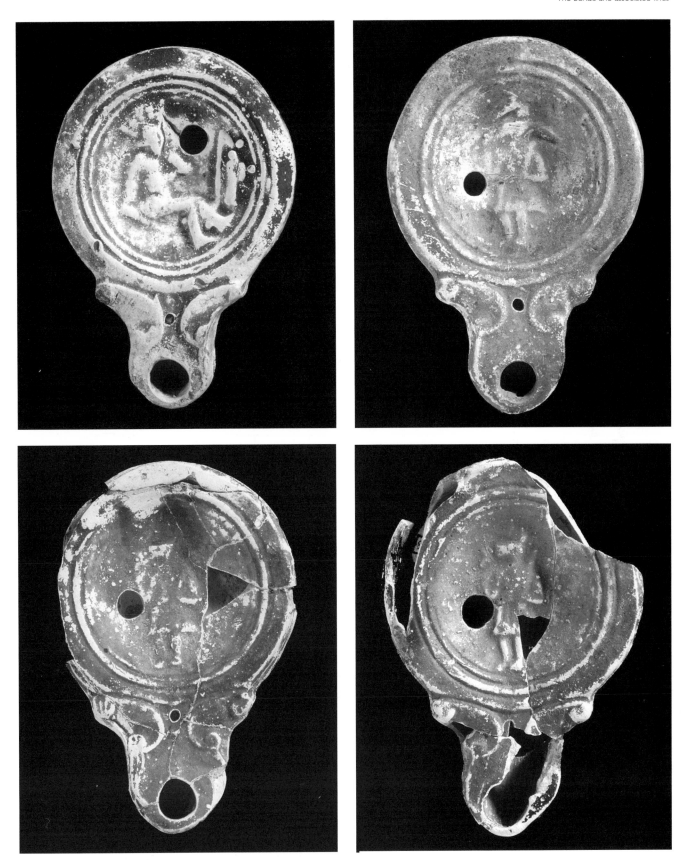

Fig 25 *The picture lamps <P1> − <P4> recovered from burial 1 (arranged clockwise from top left, scale 1:1)*

<P5> <12> [38] (Fig 26)

Firmalampe; Loeschcke Type IX. L 102; w 70; h 30mm
Complete. Three vestigial unperforated lugs; discus set off-
centre; no handle; air hole in shallow nozzle channel. There
is no trace of sooting. Fabric Central Gaulish White ware
(CGWH), patchy mid to dark brown slip.

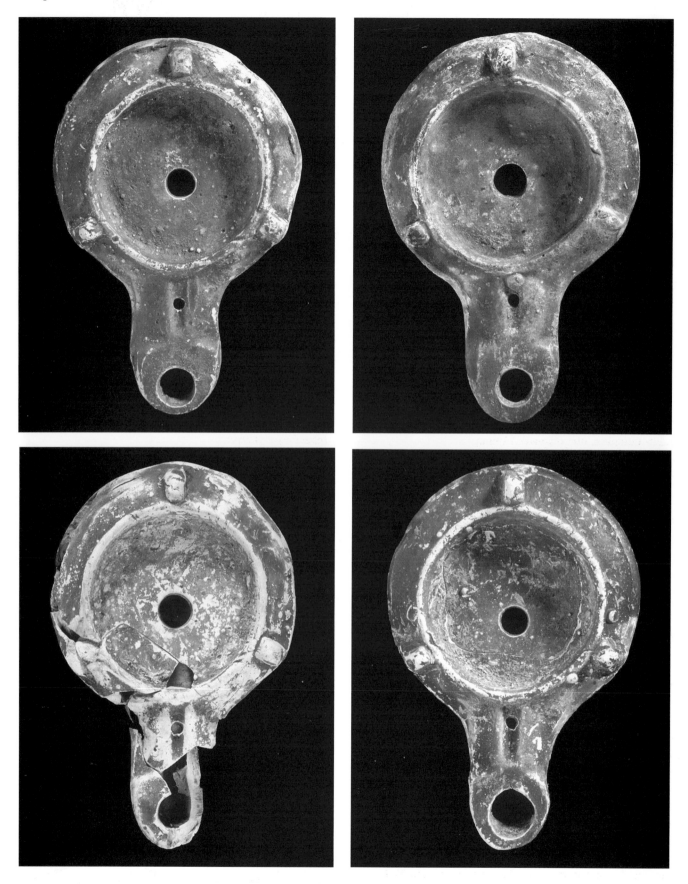

Fig 26 *The plain lamps <P5> – <P8> recovered from burial 1 (arranged clockwise from top left, scale 1:1)*

<P6> <25> [38] (Fig 26)
Firmalampe; Loeschcke Type IX. L 104; w 71; h 31mm
Complete. There are three unpierced lugs on the shoulder

and an additional one at the top of the air channel which is
pierced; central filling hole; no handle. Poorly moulded, with
the discus slightly off-centre. Fabric Central Gaulish White

ware (CGWH), with patchy dark grey to brown slip. Dark grey deposits in the area of the nozzle appear to be the remains of slip and not sooting.

<P7> <28> [38] (Fig 26)
Firmalampe; Loeschcke Type IX. L 103; w 70; h 31mm
Three unpierced lugs on the shoulder, quite sharply moulded; four irregularly spaced pellets of different sizes also on the shoulder; air hole in nozzle channel; no handle; filling hole near centre of plain discus. No signs of sooting in the nozzle. Fabric Central Gaulish White ware (CGWH), patchy mid to dark brown slip.

<P8> <29> [38] (Fig 26)
Firmalampe; Loeschcke Type IX. L c 103mm. Almost complete, although the nozzle has been broken and part of the side wall is missing. Two of three vestigial lugs are preserved; air hole in nozzle channel. Fabric Central Gaulish White ware (CGWH), very patchy grey/brown slip.

Tazze

<P9> – <P16> [38] (Figs 10 and 24)
Verulamium Region White ware fabric
<P9> Complete. Rim diameter 120mm.
<P10> Complete. 2 sherds. Rim diameter 120mm. (Fig 24)
<P11> Complete. 4 sherds. Rim diameter 125mm.
<P12> Complete. 29 sherds. Rim diameter 165mm.
<P13> Complete. 9 sherds. Rim diameter 165mm. (Fig 24)
<P14> Complete. 20 sherds. Rim diameter 120mm.
<P15> Complete. 13 sherds. Rim diameter 140mm.
<P16> Complete. 21 sherds. Rim diameter 130mm.
The vessels are quite uniform in design, all have the distinctive frill decorating the rim and carination of the body. They range in size from 120mm to 165mm in diameter and are all in the same fabric, Verulamium Region White ware (VRW).

Tazze are not uncommon finds on cremation and inhumation burial sites; 12 examples are held in Museum collections from the London cemeteries (Hall 1996, Appendix 1). Additionally, they are found in religious contexts such as the 'Triangular' temple at Verulamium (Wheeler & Wheeler 1936, 190–3, fig 32, nos 44 & 46, pl LIX) and have been found attached to triple vases, another vessel form which has ritual associations (Kaye 1914, 292, fig 10). However, the exact function is not known but it is often suggested that tazze are incense burners (Philpott 1991, 193) and all but one of the vessels at Great Dover Street had burning or sooting marks. These are on the interior and, less often, on the rim of the tazze. Only on one vessel is the base burnt (<P16>). The burning does not seem to have been severe and is unlikely to have been the cause of the vessel being broken. Neither does it seem to have been concentrated in any one area as the sooting marks tend to be irregular, often on the inside of the vessel then up one side and over the rim, as opposed to being concentrated on the bottom of the interior. These scorch marks suggest that the tazze were used outside as the wind

could cause the irregular pattern. The lack of any severe burning of the vessels supports the idea that they were possibly used only once prior to burial as has been suggested of lamps in inhumation and cremation burials elsewhere.

All but one of the vessels were broken in *situ*. The broken edges of the vessels were not abraded but neither were they fresh as the dirt was ingrained and one vessel (<P15>) had the remains of a corroded iron nail attached to a broken edge. This suggests that the vessels were broken on deposition or shortly after rather than this being a more recent event. However, the positioning of the tazze in the pit suggests that some care was taken in their deposition: 6 were inverted (2 over lamps), 2 were on their sides and 1 was upright. This argues against them having been smashed deliberately within the pit at the time of deposition as it would be very difficult to break the vessels and keep them in the same positions.

Glass

<G16> [38] <120>
Eight large fragments of fire-distorted glass. All natural green-blue glass. Indeterminate form. Damaged vessel or vessels from a funeral pyre. Roman.

Gold

[38]
Traces of gold found in the residue may be from textile (research continues).

Plant remains and animal remains

For a detailed discussion of the plant and animal remains from the *bustum*, see Giorgi *et al* in prep.

Burial 2

(Figs 11 and 27)
Inhumation burial prone
Male; 17–25 years. Caries in one of 20 surviving teeth; mild calculus on anterior lower teeth; slight periodontalism.

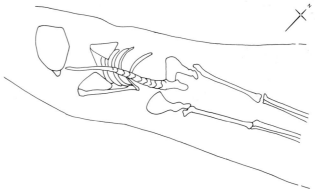

Fig 27 Plan of burial 2, a prone inhumation burial whose feet were truncated (scale 1:20)

Wormian bones on lambdoid suture. Osteoarthritis of right elbow and wrist joints, with eburnation of proximal ulna and distal radius. Fractured rib.
1st/2nd century

Glass

<G2> <63> [69]
Fragment of natural green-blue glass from a vessel of indeterminate form. Roman.

Burial 3

Inhumation burial
Adult; probably female
1st/2nd century

Burial 4

Inhumation burial
Male; 26–45 years; 171cm (5'7") tall. One out of 16 surviving teeth was affected by caries. Diffuse Idiopathic Skeletal Hyperostosis ('DISH').
Found associated with legs of a child.
1st/2nd century

Burial 5

Inhumation burial in coffin
Child; under 6 years
1st/2nd century

Burial 6

Inhumation burial in coffin
On excavation only the bones of the right arm were present. Due to their decayed condition, these could not be subjected to analysis.
?1st/2nd century

Burial 7

Inhumation burial
Adult of indeterminate sex; legs only recovered
?1st/2nd century

Burial 8

(Fig 28)
Inhumation burial possibly in coffin
Male; 26–45 years; 178cm (5'10") tall. Canine teeth in lower jaw erupted in front of lateral incisors. Slight periodontalism.
Spondylosis
In walled cemetery Structure 1, this was an extended supine inhumation, except that the cranium was found placed in the chest area. The spine was complete, the cervical vertebrae and mandible were in situ and showed no cut marks, confirming that decapitation

was not perimortal but that the cranium had been moved after the body had disintegrated by putrefactive decay.
Mid 2nd century

Ceramic

<P17> [360] BBS 2F OAL (Fig 28)
A Black-burnished-type ware everted-rim jar (BBS 2F OAL) was found to the right of the feet of the skeleton. It is decorated with burnished open acute lattice which is dated from c AD 140. The vessel is complete albeit found smashed into 134 sherds and was initially identified on site as two vessels. The surface appearance of this vessel is similar to Thameside Kent Black-burnished-type ware (TSK) which most commonly occurs in this form (Symonds & Tomber 1991, 96; Monaghan 1987, 108, nos 3J9 1–3). However, the fabric is very different under x20 magnification as the quartz is well sorted and sand-sized.

<P18> [360] <71> VRW 2T
Verulamium Region White ware necked jar (VRW 2T). This vessel is dated to c AD 50–160. The vessel was positioned above the head and to the left of the skeleton and contained a glass bottle.

Glass

<G15> [360] <121> (Fig 28)
An ovoid bottle. Free-blown; colourless glass with a greenish tint. The rim has been folded inwards and then outsplayed and flattened. The neck is cylindrical with a constriction at the base of the neck above a pear-shaped body. The base has been pushed in to form a high pointed kick. Placed inside the ceramic vessel <71> above the head and to the left of the skeleton. For a discussion of this form, see comments following <G3> in burial 26.

<G21> <47> [359] (Fig 35)
The rim of a small jar (Isings form 68). Free-blown; natural green-blue glass. Rim folded in and slightly outsplayed. Late 1st or 2nd century. Found in backfill of burial 8. For a discussion of this form, see comments following <G7> in burial 28.

Burial 9

Inhumation burial in coffin
Child; under 6 years
Mid 2nd century

Burial 10

Inhumation burial in coffin
Child; 0–5 years. Wormian bones on lambdoid suture.
Parietal osteoporosis of frontal bone.
In walled cemetery Structure 3
Mid 2nd century

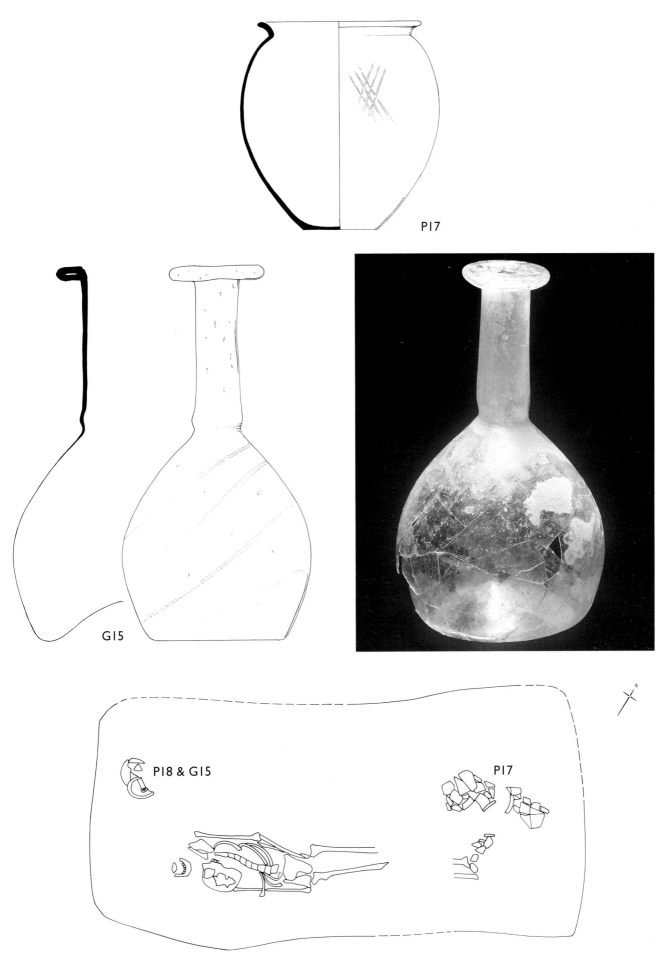

Fig 28 Plan of burial 8, an inhumation burial (scale 1:20), with illustrations of the glass vessel <G15> (scale 1:2) and the pottery vessel <P17> (scale1:4)

Burial 11

Inhumation burial in coffin
Child; 6–12 years
In walled cemetery Structure 3
Mid 2nd century

Burial 12

Inhumation burial in coffin
Adult; female. Osteoarthritis of both ankle joints
(eburnation of tali)
In walled cemetery Structure 3
Mid 2nd century

Burial 13

Cremation burial in vessel [89]
Adult of indeterminate sex
Cremation weight 0.25kg
Mid 2nd century

Burial 14

(Fig 29)
Inhumation burial possibly in coffin
Adolescent of indeterminate sex
Body lying on a bed of gravel in a stone-lined cist
Mid 2nd century

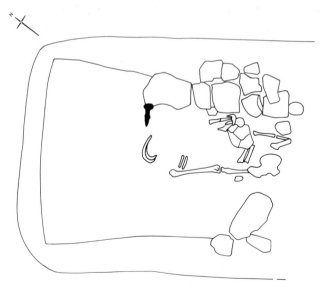

Fig 29 *Plan of burial 14, an inhumation burial within a stone-lined cist that had been robbed – a post-medieval intrusion had removed the lower half of the burial*

Burial 15

Inhumation burial in coffin
Child; under 6 years
Originally thought to be two individuals recovered from
the same grave cut, but were found to be complementary

and therefore probably comprise a single individual.
Mid 2nd century

Burial 16

Inhumation burial
Adult; female
Mid 2nd century

Iron

<S1> <93> [147] (in grave fill)
Hobnails. A triple row of nails, the exact number uncertain,
visible only on X-ray.

<S2> <90><91><92> [148]
Hobnails. An indeterminate number of hobnails, including
one very indistinct group of five, could be detected on X-ray,
representing the remains of a shoe. As feet and head area
were truncated they must have been laid alongside or on
the torso.

Burial 17

(Fig 30)
Inhumation burial in coffin
Adolescent. Wormian bones on lambdoid suture
Body laid on bed of chalk
Mid 2nd century

Ceramics

<P19> [125] NVCC 1DX (Fig 30)
A Nene Valley Colour-coated ware disc-mouthed flagon (NVCC
1DX), which was located beside the right foot of the skeleton.
This flagon is complete except for the handle and a portion of
the neck. It is slipped a reddish-brown in colour and has a
pedestal foot. The dating of this vessel is difficult because few
examples of disc-mouthed flagons from well-dated contexts
have been published. A similar vessel occurs at Colchester
(Symonds & Wade 1999, 280, fig 5.42, no. 156) but cannot
help with the dating of this type.

Burial 18

Inhumation burial
Adult male. Mild osteoarthritis of thoracic and lumbar
spine and of both elbows
?Mid 2nd century

Iron

The fragmentary and decayed remains of a pair of hobnailed
shoes were found in a small pit next to the burial. They were
recorded on site but not recovered.

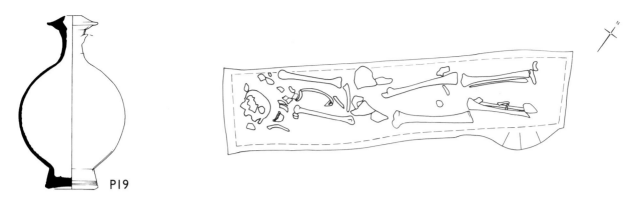

Fig 30 Plan of burial 17, an inhumation burial, laid on a bed of chalk (scale1:20) and with pottery vessel <P19> (scale 1:4)

Glass

<G1> <66> [82]
Fragment of natural green-blue glass from a vessel of indeterminate form. Roman.

Burial 19

(Fig 31)
Inhumation burial prone
Female; 17–25 years; 155cm (5'1") tall. Supracondylar process on right humerus; fifth lumbar vertebra sacralised. Two fractured ribs. Squatting facets on tibia.
Mid 2nd century

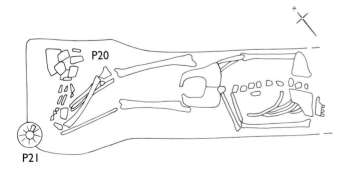

Fig 31 Plan of burial 19, a prone inhumation burial – head truncated (scale 1:20) and burial goods <P20> and <P21> (scale 1:4)

Ceramics

<P20> [164] HWC 2E BUD (Fig 31)
There was a Highgate 'C' ware round-bodied necked jar

with burnished shoulder (HWC 2E BUD) which was found smashed albeit mostly complete at the feet of the skeleton. It was thought at the time of excavation from the position of the sherds within the fill that the vessel had been deliberately smashed on deposition. The surfaces of this vessel are in a very poor condition; this can be partly explained through the vessel being badly burned but it may also be due to soil conditions. These jars are common products of this industry and are dated AD 100–60.

<P21> [164] VCWS 1B7 (Fig 31)
The second vessel found in the grave is a small example of a Verulamium Region Coarse White-slipped ware cup-mouthed ring-necked flagon (VCWS 1B7). The vessel was said to have been whole until broken during machining and was situated in the lower right corner of the grave below the feet. There is virtually no white slip left on the vessel. This may be due to soil conditions which seem to have affected the surfaces of most of the pottery on the site especially as the slip on VCWS has a tendency to be quite friable. The vessel is dated c AD 140–200.

Burial 20

Inhumation burial
Adult of indeterminate sex; 26–45 years
Mid 2nd century

Burial 21

Inhumation burial possibly in coffin
Adult of indeterminate sex. Moderate periostitis affecting both tibiae.
Mid 2nd century

Ceramics

<P22> [314] VCWS 1B7
This burial contained 19 sherds from a Verulamium Region Coarse White-slipped ware cup-mouthed ring-necked flagon (VCWS 1B7). The vessel was found broken just to the left of

the skeleton. It has not been illustrated as it is too fragmentary but is the same developed type of ring-necked flagon as that in burial 19. There are a further seven sherds in the same fabric from the backfill [313] of the grave which are probably from the same vessel. The sherd edges indicate that the flagon has not been recently broken. However, this may have occurred when the burial was disturbed and should not be seen as evidence that the vessel was deliberately smashed on deposition.

Copper alloy

<S3> <35> [314]

Brooch. Surviving l 16mm; w of head 18mm. Colchester two-piece of which only the head and the upper part of the bow survives. Spring of eight turns, incomplete. No position recorded and the fragmentary nature of the object makes it probable that it is residual.

Glass

<G12> <56> [314] (Fig 35)

The lower part of a phial (Isings form 82A2). Free-blown; natural green glass. Thin-walled with a flattened, squat body. Base decorated with 'incuso' lettering of which PATRI survives. Placed over the right leg of the skeleton. 2nd century. Probably part of grave assemblage.

Three examples of pharmaceutical or cosmetic phial are among this site assemblage (G9, G10 and G12). None is complete but each comes from a separate vessel. G10 is very fragmentary but comes from the rounded part of the body of a phial where the body has almost been flattened right down. This belongs to the general group described by Isings (1957, form 82A2/82B2) which includes the remaining two examples from Great Dover Street, which have more conical-shaped bodies. They all belong to the 2nd century, especially the middle part of that century. A bottle of similar shape from Ewer Street, Southwark is in the British Museum (Brailsford 1958, 44 no. 13 pl 12 – Acc No. 63.9–16.1).

This example, G12, is particularly interesting due to the presence on the base of a moulded inscription. Unfortunately only part of it survives but sufficient remains for it to be included among a group bearing the legend PATRIMONI, or VECTIGAL PATRIMONI, in full or abbreviated. According to CIL (Corpus inscriptionum latinarum) there are 14 examples of this type of legend recorded in Rome, 2 in Etruria, 6 in Gaul, 1 in Germany and at least 4 in Britain. The precise interpretation of the legend is in doubt. It is universally agreed that it relates to an Imperial Estate, or rather the validation of the products from an Imperial Estate. Baldacci has suggested that the legend related to products from Judaea (Judaean Balsam) but as one can see from the distribution it is a western form (Baldacci 1969, 353). Dessau suggested that the word 'vectigal' (implying property of the state) would have secured tax-free entry at a provincial frontier fort for the contents of the bottle. However, this interpretation is flawed because such

an arrangement could easily be abused as the bottles could be reused by third parties (Price 1977, 31). Perhaps it is easier to say, simply, that the bottle originally carried products (probably an expensive cosmetic or, less likely, a pharmaceutical preparation) which had been made by a state-owned property. The origin of this item is uncertain, but it is most likely to be Italian.

Burial 22

(Fig 32)
Inhumation burial
Female; 17–25 years; 153cm (5'0") tall. Bilateral septal apertures to humerus.
Found associated with burial 23
Mid 2nd century

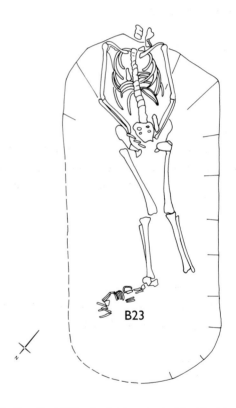

Fig 32 Plan of burial 22, a female inhumation burial, with a baby, burial 23, at her foot (scale 1:20, see also Fig 20)

Glass

<G13> <13> [324] (Fig 37)

Glass counter; dia 14.7mm. A deep blue, plano-convex; abraded. In grave fill, position not recorded, probably part of the grave assemblage.

<G14> <94> [325]

Two very small fragments of fire-damaged glass. Probably waste or loose fragments from a disturbed cremation or funeral pyre. Indeterminate colour and form.

Iron

<S4> <88> [325]
Scatter of eight hobnails, possibly in situ and representing a shoe. No nail pattern recoverable. Placed over left side of pelvis, an unusual position for a shoe, but footwear was frequently placed in positions other than at the foot of the grave.

Burial 23

(Fig 32)
Inhumation burial
Neonate
Found at the foot of burial 22
Mid 2nd century

Burial 24

Cremation burial in vessel [52]
Adult male
Cremation weight 1.58kg
Mid 2nd century

Ceramics

<P23> [52] BB1 2
Only the base of this vessel, Black-burnished-type 1 ware jar (BB1 2), was present and is in 38 sherds. As no decoration is present further refinement beyond the overall dates of the fabric is not possible.

Burial 25

(Fig 33)
Inhumation burial in coffin
Male; 17–25 years. Caries in one of 14 surviving teeth. Fusion of first and second right cuneiforms. Compound fracture of left tibia and fibula.
Body packed with chalk
Late 2nd/3rd century

Glass

<G4> <50> [160] (Fig 35)
The base of an 'Airlie' type beaker (Isings form 85b). Free-blown; colourless glass. Hollow tubular base-ring with a central solid ring. Late 2nd or early 3rd century. Possibly intentionally placed in the grave as a disc (ie pendant?) rather than a vessel part.

The 'Airlie' cup (Barber & Bowsher 2000, 255) is another distinctive vessel which first appears during the second half of the 2nd century, the earliest example from Britain coming from a pit at Felmongers Lane, Harlow (Price 1987, 192, fig 2.19), and continues to be produced into the first half of the 3rd century (Isings 1957, form 85). This cylindrical form with a thickened inward sloping rim and an applied ring of glass

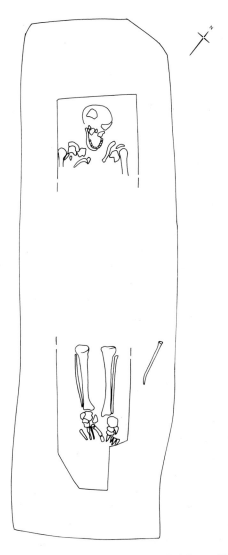

Fig 33 Plan of burial 25, an inhumation burial packed with chalk – middle of burial truncated (scale1:20)

inside the base-ring (Isings 1957, form 85b) is well attested throughout the north-western provinces in contexts of this date, for example a minimum of 39 examples alone came from Colchester (Cool & Price 1995, 82).

It is interesting to note that only the distinctive base part of this particular vessel was found here. Of course, this being the thickest part of the 'Airlie' beaker, together with the rim, this may be merely coincidental. However, with the context of the find-spot in mind, it may be possible that this part had been intentionally selected. There is little evidence for grozing around the extremities which normally accompanies such items selected for use as gaming counters or pendants, but the body parts have been broken off very close to the base-ring. It is just possible, therefore, that this item functioned as a disc of some sort. Whether this was as a gaming counter or talisman/pendant is, considering the uncertainty of this hypothesis, just too speculative.

<G5> <49> [160]
Fragment of greenish-blue glass from a vessel of indeterminate form. Roman.

Burial 26

(Fig 34)
Inhumation burial in coffin
Child; 6–12 years. Rachitic skeleton
Body packed with chalk
Late 2nd/3rd century

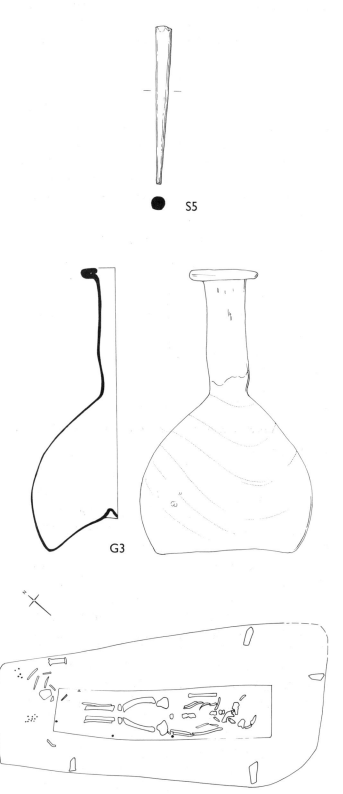

S5

G3

Fig 34 *Plan of burial 26, an inhumation burial packed with chalk (scale 1:20), and associated burial goods <G3> (scale 1:2) and <S5> (scale 1:1)*

Glass

<G3> <27> [151] (Fig 34)
A pyriform flask. Free-blown; natural green-blue glass. Rim folded in and flattened. Thin-walled, pear-shaped body with a narrow neck, constricted at the junction of neck and body. Pushed-in base with a pointed kick. 2nd or 3rd century. Placed at the foot of the grave, below and to the right of the right foot.

Another flask broadly similar to this, but slightly larger and different in colour, comes from burial 8 <G15> (see Fig 28). Two others come from graves postdating the middle of the 3rd century in the east London cemetery area (MSL87 Burial 392, [745] <358> and SCS83 Burial 4, [111] <5>; Barber & Bowsher 2000). Both are colourless with greenish tints, more similar in this respect to <G15>.

There are numerous ovoid, pear-shaped or pyriform-shaped flasks among Roman glass repertoires from the first introduction of glass blowing during the 1st century BC through to the 4th or 5th century. The shape is, in effect, the natural shape of an inflated paraison of glass – the neck being formed simply by allowing the mass of the body to sag and thus stretch the upper part of the paraison closest to the blowing-iron. It is not surprising, therefore, to find that there are numerous references to such vessels throughout the Roman Empire. This being so, it is interesting to note that there are a number of subtle differences between individual examples, such as neck width in proportion to the body size, the shape of the body profile (eg from straight to curved), the finish of the base (eg presence/absence of basal kick and, if present, the height of this kick), presence or absence of neck/body constriction and, of significance for functional purposes, the actual size (therefore, volume) of individual examples. It should also be noted that the rim forms of these vessels are the same as those for other bottle and flask types. It is therefore probable that this form was more common in Londinium than the few complete examples would suggest.

In Britain, the form is known in a pre-Boudican layer at Sheepen (Harden 1947, 304 no. 83, pl 88). This example is more similar to <G3> than <G15>, being blue-green in colour. However, it has a folded triangular rim and a low, pushed-in base. In general, such flasks or bottles with broad, almost horizontal rims and high pushed-in bases such as these two examples date from the 2nd century onwards. Also, the metal of <G15>, colourless glass with a greenish tint, conforms to the dates of similarly coloured examples. A colourless vessel came from Infirmary Fields, Chester in a mid to late 2nd-century context (Newstead 1914, 126, pl 31, fig 1) and a bottle in a greenish metal came from a late Roman burial at Cirencester (McWhirr et al 1982, 132, fig 81.356).

A number of similar bottles are known; for instance a bottle similar to <G15>, with a narrower neck and more pronounced constriction, and dating to the 2nd or 3rd century came from Bonn (Follman-Schulz 1988, 24). Four others which compare generally with <G15> from Bonn date from the first half of the 3rd century to the 4th century (Follman-

Schulz 1988, 28–9, nos 44–7). A late 2nd- or early 3rd-century vessel came from Poitiers (Lantier 1929, 11, pl 12b); a bottle very similar to <G12>, dated to the late 3rd or 4th century, came from an inhumation at Maldon Road, Colchester (Cool & Price 1995, 150–1, no. 1176), and a 4th-century bottle came from Intercisa in a 4th-century grave (Vago & Bona 1976, Grave 174, table 10).

Jet

<S5> <34> [151] (Fig 34)

Incomplete pin; l 41.5mm. Lower part of tapering shank. Without the head it is impossible to state to which type this belongs, but the most common type, seen elsewhere in London, has a faceted cube head, for example as at burials in the eastern cemetery where hairpins were found next to the head (Barber & Bowsher 2000, 160, 216). Found to the right of the right leg, above the ankle, in the grave fill. This may have been used as a shroud pin. Its incomplete state and position in the grave fill raises the possibility that it was redeposited. Possibly 3rd/4th century.

Iron

Hobnails were observed on site, but only as staining and it was not possible to lift them. They were in two groups at the foot of the grave and represent unworn footwear.

Animal bone

The skeleton of a chicken was found at the foot of the grave. The chicken skeleton comprised 14 fragments. It was not stated whether this skeleton was articulated or disarticulated when found. However, it is notable that both tarsometatarsi, as well as the posterior phalanges, are absent. In addition both tibiotarsi are broken at the midshaft (fresh breakage), each then represented by proximal end fragments. The absence of such a specific range of bones strongly suggests that the skeleton was articulated, and that these hindleg parts had been removed from the rest of the skeleton for whatever reason. It is perhaps likely that the fresh breaks indicate that these bones were lost during excavation. This skeleton was undoubtedly carefully excavated, once it was recognised as a possible burial good; however, no attempt was made to sieve the surrounding soil for the missing skeletal parts.

The significance of its state of articulation concerns the interpretation of the type of burial good represented. A whole articulated skeleton clearly suggests that the offering consisted of an entire chicken. The absence of any obvious butchery marks provides further proof of the entirety of this bird when deposited. All the long-bone epiphyses are fused indicating an adult bird, while the presence of medullary bone (see Driver 1982) shows that it was female. The bird used may therefore have been an old boiler, that is, a hen which was either surplus to, or no longer able to be used for, egg production.

There is a similarity between this site and the eastern

cemetery, in that very few inhumation burials produced animal burial goods (Barber & Bowsher 2000, 130–3). This is in sharp contrast to the human cremations found at the latter sites, a very large proportion of which contained burnt animal bones. The use of chicken as some kind of offering has parallels within the inhumation and cremation burials at the eastern cemetery sites, this species occurring in 15 out of 19 inhumation burials, and in 28 out of a total of 77 cremation burials, with animal burial goods. In both types of burial, there are instances, perhaps more abundant within cremation burials, of the use of whole birds.

A general review of the use of animal burial goods throughout the Roman period has been put together by Philpott (1991). He describes a number of inhumations from south-east England, many of which contained animal burial goods, with chicken frequently used among quite a wide array of animal and bird species. As at the eastern cemetery, chicken remains were also very often present among the cremation burials from these sites, and again, there is good evidence for the use of entire carcasses.

Burial 27

Inhumation burial in coffin
Female; 26–45 years. Caries in four of 16 surviving teeth. Incipient Diffuse Idiopathic Skeletal Hyperostosis ('DISH'); osteoarthritis of ankle joint.
Body packed with chalk
Late 2nd/3rd century

Burial 28

Cremation burial
Young adult of indeterminate sex; 17–25 years
A grave-shaped cut contained a large amount of smashed pottery and glass; the cremation [291] (weight 0.50kg) was found associated with the pottery vessels but it is not possible to determine which one, if any, it was originally placed in.
Possibly 3rd century

Ceramics

A large group of pottery was retrieved from this burial. No whole vessels were recovered; however, semi-complete albeit broken vessels were found. The group is particularly badly abraded and some of the sherds may be from the backfill of the grave rather than vessels associated with the burial or cremation. The broken edges of the majority of the sherds are not fresh indicating that the vessels were not broken recently. The most complete vessel was <P55>, a Colour-coated ware bag-shaped beaker, with cornice rim and clay pellet roughcast decoration (CC 3J CR, RCD2). Diameter 85mm (Fig 37).

The vessels listed below are possible burial or cremation vessels. Due to the level of abrasion and their fragmentary condition they have not been illustrated but references have been given for published examples. Other forms present within the group but only represented by one or two diagnostic sherds include two reduced Sand-tempered ware lids (SAND 9A) and the base of a Moselkeramik beaker with indentations (MOSL 3 UND). The group is dated on this one sherd of MOSL to AD 200–75. However, the rest of the assemblage could be dated to the second half of the 2nd century.

1) Black-burnished-type ware everted-rim jar with open acute-lattice decoration (BBS 2F OAL). Diameter range from 150mm to 195mm.

    There were a total of 154 sherds and at least four vessels are represented here. The surfaces and edges of sherds are damaged. There were two lower halves of jars, probably an everted-rim jar (2F). Some of the sherds have surfaces which are similar to the fabric described as Thameside Kent Black-burnished-type ware (TSK), but the fabric is different, being composed of well-sorted sand-sized quartz.

2) Verulamium Region Coarse White-slipped ware necked jar (VCWS 2T) (Davies et al 1994, 59, fig 47, no. 264). Diameter c 170mm.

3) Verulamium Region White ware necked jar (VRW 2T).

Diameter 170mm. Same form as above.

4) Verulamium Region White ware 'honey pot' jar (VRW 2K) (Davies et al 1994, fig 47, no. 264). Diameter 120mm. The vessel is also lightly ribbed.

5) Oxidised ware lid (OXID 9A). Diameter 150mm. Rim is folded back to form bead.

6) Black-burnished-type 2 ware dish with simple rim with wavy line decoration (BB2 5J WL) (Symonds & Tomber 1994, 71, fig 51, no. 37). Diameter 195mm.

7) Black-burnished-style ware rounded-rim bowl (BBS 4H). Diameter 230mm.

Glass

All the glass vessels are fragmentary and it is possible that all are associated with disturbed cremation burials.

<G6> <44> <64> [291] (Fig 35)
The rim, part of the side and part of the base of an urn (Isings form 67a). Free-blown; natural green-blue glass. Rim folded inwards and flattened out to form a broad hollow-tubular rim.

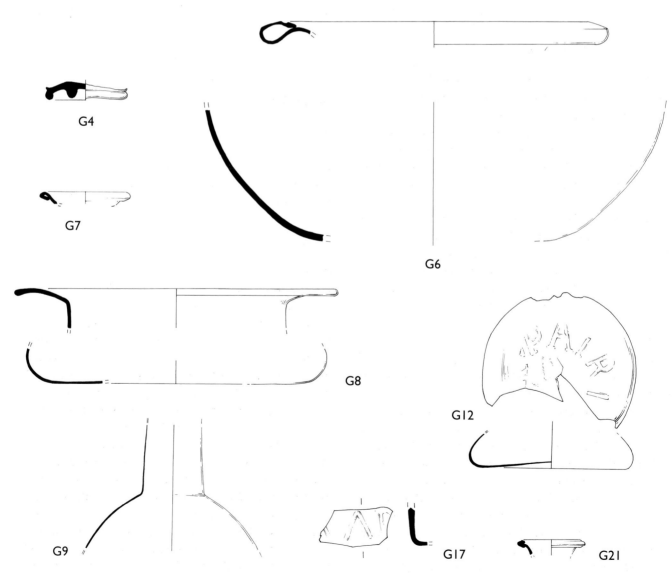

Fig 35 *Glass vessels <G4>, <G6>, <G7>, <G8>, <G9>, <G12>, <G17> and <G21> (scale 1:2)*

Bulbous body with a slightly pushed-in base. The rim of this vessel is complete (though broken) but only a small proportion of the body and base survives. Late 1st or 2nd century. This may be part of the primary fill, but is more likely to be residual from a disturbed cremation which, most likely, was previously located in the vicinity of burial 28.

This form, with a sturdy horizontal rim, is a frequent discovery in cremation contexts and there is a possibility that many were made specifically for that function. Considering the thickness of the rim, and the preferential survival of such large parts in the archaeological record, it is perhaps significant that none has been found in ordinary occupation levels in London and Southwark. Furthermore, there are no fragments from the rims of these jars among the large (50kg) cullet deposit found in 1996 at Guildhall Yard (GYE92 [14319]). This dump of broken glass, abandoned for some unknown reason from a glass workshop in the Guildhall/Upper Walbrook area, dates to the first quarter of the 2nd century, contemporary with these urns, and contains a wide range of vessel types of that era, and some from earlier repertoires.

This vessel <G6> is very thick-walled for its type and is in a poor-quality glass. The mass of seed (gas/air bubbles), batch (undissolved solid material) and waste clay fragments (picked up during second gathers and working of the paraison) is not a common feature of these vessels. It is tempting to suggest that this particular example may not have travelled very far from its place of manufacture. Furthermore, the rim form, folded inwards and flattened out, is not consistent with the greater majority of examples throughout the western Empire which have their rims rolled outwards (eg Dilly & Mahéo 1997, 63, nos 1–5, pl 1). In the light of the comment made immediately above about the place of manufacture of this example, it may be of significance therefore to note that two examples which have similar rim forms come from Bishopsgate (found 1873 as part of a cinerary group with a Dr27 samian cup, a square-sectioned glass bottle and a small glass phial – RCHME 1928, 159, fig 65, 32, MoL Acc No. A14400) and Southwark (site not stated – RCHME 1928, 169, fig 69, 63).

<G7> <45> [291] (Fig 35)
Fragment from the rim of a small jar (Isings form 68). Free-blown; natural green-blue glass. Rim folded in and slightly outsplayed. Late 1st or 2nd century.

A similar rim fragment <G21> came from the backfill of burial 8. Other exact parallels from London come from West Tenter Street (Jones 1986, fig 38.4) in a cremation dated c AD 120–80 and Mansell Street (Barber & Bowsher 2000, Burial 197, <67>). The form (Isings 1957, form 68) is a miniature version of the standard late 1st- or 2nd-century jar (Isings 1957, form 67) and would have been used for cosmetic or pharmaceutical preparations. Other dated examples come from Trier (second half of the 1st century – Goethert-Polaschek 1977, 242, nos 1440 & 1441, tables 10.118k, 6.72b) and Housesteads (2nd century – Charlesworth 1971, fig 10).

<G8> <39> [291] (Fig 35)
Part of the rim, side and base of a necked jar. Free-blown; colourless glass with a greenish tint. Rim fire-rounded and folded outwards. The neck tapers slightly in towards the rim. The body is a flattened cone, with a slightly pushed-in base. Late 2nd or 3rd century. The comment for <G6> above applies here also.

<G9> <41> [291] (Fig 35)
Part of the neck and body of a phial (Isings form 82A2). Free-blown; natural green-blue glass. Thin-walled, squat body. Pushed-in base. Late 1st or 2nd century. The comment for <G6> above applies here also. For a brief discussion of this type, see the comments for <G12> above.

<G10> <40> [291]
Fragment of natural green glass from the lower part of a flask or phial. The comment for <G6> above applies here also. For a brief discussion of this type, see the comments for <G12> above (burial 21).

<G11> <42> [291]
Fragment of colourless glass from the body of a ?beaker of indeterminate form.

Burial 29

(Fig 36)
Inhumation burial
Child; 6–12 years. Metopic suture
Latest burial in walled cemetery Structure 3
Mid 3rd century

Ceramics

<P24> [122] NVCC 3K END (Fig 36)
This is a Nene Valley Colour-coated ware globular necked beaker (NVCC 3K END). The vessel although complete is broken into 20 sherds; this may have occurred post-deposition as there is evidence the burial had been disturbed. The beaker was located to the east of the lower limbs of the skeleton. It is decorated with six elongated indentations and three bands of rouletting and is slipped with an uneven brown-orange wash. There is possibly some slight sooting on the exterior of the vessel. It also has a bead rim and a tall narrow neck. Similar vessels albeit with plain rims illustrated in the summary of the industry (Howe et al 1980, 18, fig 4, nos 42–3) are dated to the mid to late 3rd century. Identical parallels are found at Colchester (Symonds & Wade in prep, 280, fig 5.39, nos 50–4) which have beaded rims and the same number of bands of rouletting. Two of the Colchester examples occur in groups which have end dates of c AD 250 and c AD 300. Overall the evidence suggests that this vessel dates to the mid to late 3rd century.

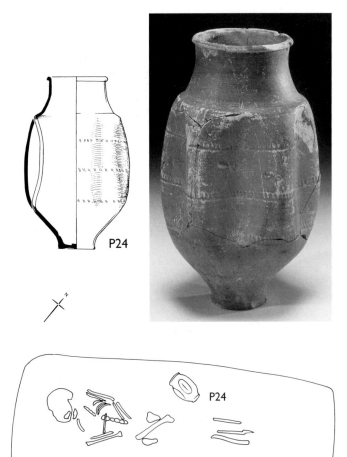

Fig 36 Plan of burial 29, an inhumation burial (scale 1:20), with grave good <P24> (scale 1:4)

Burial 30

Cremation burial in vessel [48]
Adult; male, elderly, aged over 45 years
Cremation weight 1.10kg
Mid 3rd century

Ceramics

<P25> <102> [48] AHFA 2 COMB (Fig 37)
This is an Alice Holt Farnham storage jar with combed herringbone decoration (AHFA 2 COMB). The vessel is broken into 48 sherds and is incomplete as the rim is missing. There is post-firing graffito on the shoulder of the vessel. The graffito is retrograde and reads I I I I X X X, which translates as '34'. This perhaps refers to a measure of the jar's contents such as the weight, volume or number of items (Mark Hassall, pers comm). If the graffito does refer to the capacity of the vessel then this suggests that the jar is reused and that the first use of the vessel was for storage.

4.2 Probable displaced burial goods

Ceramics

<P26> <3> [319] (Fig 37)
Firmalampe; Loeschcke Type IX. L 89.5; w 50; h 27mm
Complete. Two vestigial unpierced lugs on the shoulder; filling hole at the front of the plain discus; integral ring handle. Oxidised fabric. The small size of this lamp suggests that it may have been manufactured especially for funerary rather than practical use. The thickness of the wall seen at the wick hole, at least 4mm, indicates that the oil reservoir was extremely small and there is no sign of sooting around the nozzle. Found in a brickearth deposit outside Structure 1.

<P27> <52> [79]
Small *Firmalampe*; Loeschcke Type IX. L 77; w 48; h 22.5mm
Incomplete; most of the base, part of one side and half the nozzle missing. One vestigial lug, consisting of a small ball of clay, remains on the intact side. This would have been matched on the other side and there is another on the discus, just above the filling hole. The lamp had an integral ring handle, of which only part survives. There is no sign of sooting. Very coarse Local Oxidised fabric (LOXI). Found in a Roman pit, Watching Brief 1.

<P28> <69> [67]
Incomplete; three small fragments of side wall and discus from a closed lamp. Lyon ware, very abraded. Residual from a post-medieval pit.

<P29> <10> [333] OXID 9F (Fig 16)
An Oxidised ware tettina (OXID 9F) was found complete except for two small chips to the rim and one to the foot pad. The fabric is an unsourced oxidised ware and light cream in colour. It has a short constricted neck and a slightly flaring rim and there is a small spout on the body of the vessel which is also marked with a girth groove. The form is 78mm in height and has a maximum width of 84mm. Patches of what may be burning on the foot and one side of the lower body suggest that the vessel has possibly been exposed to a fire.

Tettinae vary in form and fabric and no exact parallel has been found for this example. As well as coarse wares they also occur in fine imported fabrics such as Central Gaulish Glazed ware and Central Gaulish samian (Greene 1979, 95; Webster 1981) and also in glass. Glass examples such as Isings form 99 (Isings 1957, 118) resemble jugs with an applied spout on the body. But despite the differences in form between the glass and ceramic examples, the positioning of the small distinctive spout on the widest point of each vessel suggests that they share the same function. They are uncommon finds on Roman sites in London, with only one example listed from a cemetery in a Museum of London collection (Hall 1996, Appendix 1) compared to a total of 12 recorded from graves

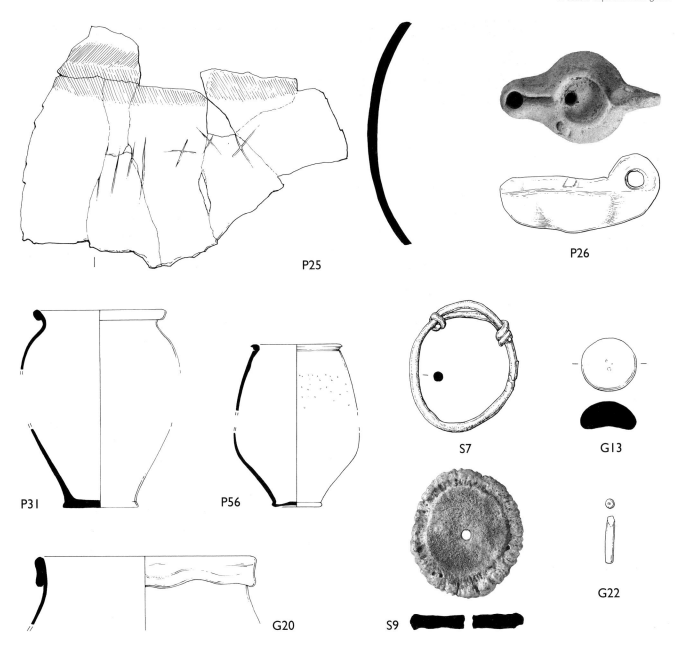

Fig 37 Pottery vessels <P25>, <P26>, <P31> and <P56> (scale 1:4 except <P26> 1:2), glass vessels <G13> (scale 1:1), <G20> (scale 1:2) and <G22> (scale 1:1), and small finds <S7> (scale 1:1) and <S9> (scale 1:2)

in Colchester (Crummy et al 1993, 273). They are quite rare in non-cemetery assemblages from the City and Southwark but this may be partly due to the difficulty in identifying the form from broken sherds as the only diagnostic feature is the spout which can be quite small. Although tettinae are often referred to as babies' feeding bottles this definition has been widely questioned (eg Isings 1957, 118; Greene 1979, 95; Webster 1981, 251–3; Martin 1997, 281–2). Other suggested possible uses have included weaning bottles, invalid cups, lamp fillers and vessels used to trail slip in samian production.

In view of the number of burials within the area and the completeness of the tettina it is highly likely that it was originally associated with a burial. Found in a brickearth deposit within Structure 1.

Copper alloy

<S6> <21> [190]

Brooch. L 39mm. Almost complete with damaged head. Colchester two-piece, with two parallel grooves at the end of each wing, mouldings and a crest on the bow. The spring is corroded but probably had six turns; pin missing.

Apart from slight damage the brooch is in good condition. It was found in the robbing of the outer wall of the walled cemetery Structure 1, but cannot be associated with any specific burial. It is however the type of object frequently found in burials, either worn on the person or deposited as a grave offering and it is highly likely that it is a residual or disturbed burial good.

<S7> <36> [226] (Fig 37)
Bracelet. Dia 30.5mm; internal dia oval 24mm x 26mm.
Small bracelet of the expanding, sliding knot type, in which
the terminals are twisted back around the hoop. Its small size
suggests that it was intended for an infant or young child, and
there is a bracelet of similar size among a group in a burial
from the eastern cemetery (B461, Barber & Bowsher 2000,
199). The form is very similar to an earring of Allason-Jones
Type 3 (Allason-Jones 1989a, fig 1, 3), which was probably
intended for permanent insertion in the ear (see also Crummy
1983, 50, no. 798, fig 53) and can also be confused with rings
for holding chatelaines (Crummy 1983, 62, no. 1945).
Allason-Jones points out that earrings tend to be finer and
more carefully made chatelaine rings with a marked taper at
the terminals (1989a, 6). The gauge of the Great Dover Street
example is 3mm, rather coarse for an earring, with only a
slight thinning at the coiled terminals. The twisted fastening
is also very secure and it seems more probable that the object
is a child's bracelet than an earring. From a brickearth deposit
within S3.

Glass

<G17> <65> [366] (Fig 35)
Fragment from the base and side of a prismatic, square-
sectioned bottle (Isings form 50). Mould-blown; natural
green-blue glass. Base decorated with a legend, of which just
AAI, or IVV, survive. Late 1st or 2nd century. Found in fill
of a possible grave near burials 6 and 7.

The square-sectioned bottle (Isings 1957, form 50) is
one of the most common vessel types among Roman glass
repertoires of the late 1st to early 3rd centuries. They had a
multitude of functions, primarily as transit or storage
containers for liquid and semi-viscous foodstuffs and cosmetics.
The larger examples, some of which stand above 30cm in
height, were also used as cinerary urns (eg Blomfield Street,
London – RCHME 1928, 161, fig 66, no. 35i) and smaller
vessels were included not as offerings in their own right but
as the containers of liquids etc to provide the soul of the
deceased on their journey. The greater proportion of these
bottles have some form of basal marking, the most common
of which are concentric circles. This vessel has the remains of
a lettered design. These are not common and tend to consist
of, mainly, abbreviated names of individuals or towns. This
example appears to be part of a name but, frustratingly, it
cannot be matched to any other known example.

<G18> <19> [52]
Fragment from the side of a large prismatic, square-sectioned
vessel, probably a bottle (Isings form 50). Mould-blown;
natural green-blue glass. Late 1st to 3rd centuries. Found near
burial 24. See the general comments for G17 above.

<G19> <33> [113]
Fragment from the side of a large prismatic, square-sectioned
vessel, probably a bottle (Isings form 50). Mould-blown;

natural green-blue glass. Late 1st to 3rd centuries. Found in
possible marking-out ditch. See the general comments for
G17 above.

<G20> <26> [182] (Fig 37)
Two fragments from the rim of, most probably, a prismatic,
square-sectioned jar (Isings form 62). Mould-blown; natural
green-blue glass. Thick rim, folded out and down to form a
broad collared rim. Late 1st or 2nd century. Probably part of
a disturbed cremation. Found in possible marking-out ditch.

The square-sectioned jar is a very close relative to the bottle
form described above (G17–19). The technique of manufacture
is essentially the same except that one is finished with a tall,
narrow neck whereas the other has a squat, wide mouth similar
to the bulbous jar (Isings 1957, form 67c). These too would
have been used as containers. Unfortunately, although it is
likely that they were very common, identifying them is not
easy from body fragments or rim fragments alone as they can
be confused with the similar looking elements from the square
bottles (Isings 1957, form 50) and bulbous jars (Isings 1957,
form 67c) respectively. This example, being very large, is most
likely to have been used in the vicinity as a cinerary urn before
its deposition outside a burial context. Other jars from burial
contexts come from, for example, Cirencester (Kingsmead –
Thorpe 1935, 5, pl 2c), Chichester (Down & Rule 1971, 99,
fig 5.22/79e) and Mancetter (Price 1982, 134, no. 1 fig 2).

<G22> <55> [104] (Fig 37)
Complete bead. L 23mm; dia 2.5mm. Cylindrical; opaque.
Found in a brickearth deposit outside Structure 3.

Antler

<S8> <9> [374]
'Toggle'. L 95mm; w 25mm
Tube, tapering slightly at each end. In the centre a sub-
rectangular hole, 21mm x 10mm, perforates both sides of
the object and on either side of the hole are parallel grooves
with decorative hatching inside, the surface very worn. There
are traces of brown ?pigment on the surface. It belongs to a
class of objects generally called 'toggles' but their precise
function is as yet unknown. They occur most commonly in
Iron Age contexts but continue into the early Roman period,
for example as at Castleford (Greep 1998, 283, nos 186–8).
Found in possible grave cut beneath burial 8 in walled
cemetery Structure 1.

<S9> <112> [53] (Fig 37)
Pendant. Dimensions 65mm x 61mm; thickness 9mm. Antler
roundel, sawn from the skull, where cuts are visible on one
side. The outer face shows the natural surface of the antler
crown and is pierced with a central hole, diameter 6mm.

This belongs to a class of pendants, made from the crown
or burr of red deer antler, which are widely known in the
north-western Roman provinces, particularly from early
Roman contexts. Several forms are known, ranging from a

simple roundel to more elaborate examples sometimes carved with a phallus (Greep 1994, 80, fig 1). Our pendant belongs to Greep's Type 2, which has a perforated central field, and the suggestion is made that the hole could have been intended for the insertion of a separate, carved phallus, although no examples have been found in situ. If it was worn as an amulet the central hole would be suitable for a cord or thong and there is now certainly sufficient evidence available to discount earlier interpretations of these objects as spindlewhorls (eg MacGregor 1985, 187). Some of the more elaborate amulets were attached to a backing by means of copper-alloy rivets and one from London has plaster adhering to the back, suggesting that it was affixed to a wall (Greep 1994, 85). Undecorated pendants have the widest distribution, but Greep has noted some variation in the distribution of the more elaborate types (1994, 87). London has already produced five examples of the latter, and although the plain types are in general more common, this is the first Type 2 recorded from the City and Southwark. Several of the pendants from Britain and France listed by Greep were found in burials, those from cremations, as at Besançon (Hatt et al 1955; Béal 1983), placed in the grave after the body had been burned. (The significance of antler pendants and their place in burials is discussed in 3.2 above). Found in the infilled possible marking-out ditch.

4.3 Artefacts from non-burial contexts

Ceramics

<P30> [304] GAUL1 8G4 (Fig 38)
An amphora was found within Structure 1 buried upright, its neck apparently protruding above the original ground surface. A substantial proportion of this vessel, a Gauloise type 4 amphora (GAUL1 8G4), is present, the foot and body are complete although most of the top part from the neck upwards is missing with only a few fragments of the rim and handle being found inside. On site the amphora was found to contain a large collection of iron nails and although it was initially thought to contain a cremation no human bone was found on excavation in the laboratory. It is not possible to say whether the form was complete at time of burial although the rim and handle sherds found inside the vessel suggest that this may have been the case, possibly with damage occurring to the amphora on burial or from later activity. The form is dated c AD 150–250 on its narrow foot, a feature which is thought to have chronological significance (Dangréaux & Desbat 1988, 128–9, fig 8, d). It has been suggested that the vessel was buried with the neck above ground level to receive libations during the parentalia, the festival of the dead.

The amphora, which was excavated in the laboratory, contained 52 nails of varying sizes on many of which were preserved traces of carbonised and mineral-replaced wood. The direction of the wood grain was recorded and although

in many cases the fragments are small and the grain not consistent in direction along a single shaft, sufficient remains for consideration of the possibility that the amphora contained a nailed box or other wooden object. The positions of the nails were planned as the amphora was excavated. Many were poorly preserved, but where recognisable were Manning Type 1 (1985, 134), with a square-sectioned tapering stem and a flat round or sub-rectangular head. The largest nails, up to 80mm in length, were found in the top half of the amphora, placed around the edge of the vessel, with a concentration on one side (nails 1–26). The size of the nails appeared to decrease towards the base of the vessel, but they were less well preserved and most were fragmentary. These fragments were spread over the whole area of the vessel. The available evidence has not permitted an attempt at reconstruction and it is possible that the wooden container was burned before being placed in the amphora. The fill contained many small fragments of charred wood which were found at many different angles. Other problems are the size of some of the nails, which appear to be rather large for a casket, and the absence of any other metal fittings which might be expected. With the exception of the nails no objects were found within the residue nor was any cremated bone.

<P31> [245] SAND 2T (Fig 37)
'Votive vessel'. Sand-tempered ware necked jar (SAND 2T), incomplete and broken into 13 sherds. The surfaces are a medium grey in colour with patches of orange as if burnt.

Fig 38 Amphora <P30> found within Structure 1, after excavation and conservation

The vessel is poorly finished with extraneous lumps of clay from the base lapping over on to the lower part of the body. The surface appearance is not dissimilar to that of Thameside Kent Black-burnished-type ware (TSK) (Symonds & Tomber 1994, 96) and the form is similar to the globular-necked jars which that industry produces. However, under microscopic examination the fabric is not the same as that described as TSK. Found close to the possible mausoleum Structure 2.

Glass

<G23> <32> [293]
Fragment of natural green-blue window glass of the cast matt/glossy variety. Roman. Found in backfill to large robbed feature in Structure 1.

Stone

quern
<76> [134]
Dia 380mm; h 90mm. Greensand. Fragment of upper stone, about 20% present. The grinding surface is very worn, but there are traces of radial grooving. The stone may have been reused as there are deep vertical cuts on one of the broken edges and on the broken hopper, also cuts on the upper surface of the domed stone. The use of this type of stone reinforces evidence for contact with the Kent area as a source of supply (Susan Pringle, pers comm).

hone
<109> [234]
L 88mm; incomplete. Part of a very abraded hone in a coarse-grained grey sandstone. One end is complete, the other, where it has been worn thin with use, is broken.

Table 5 Catalogue of inhumation and cremation burials

Burial	Context	Sex	Age (yrs)	Head	Coffin	Goods	Date (later than)
[b1]*	38	female	adult	–	–	yes	1st/2nd c
[b2]	70	male	17-25	SW	–	–	1st/2nd c
[b3]	102	? female	adult	NW	–	–	1st/2nd c
[b4]	65	male	26-45	SW	–	–	1st/2nd c
[b5]	281	–	0-5	SW	yes	–	1st/2nd c
[b6]	286	–	?	SE	yes	–	?1st/2nd c
[b7]	221	–	adult	SW	–	–	?1st/2nd c
[b8]	360	male	26-45	SW	?	yes	mid 2nd c
[b9]	296	–	0-5	NW	yes	–	mid 2nd c
[b10]	156	–	0-5	SW	yes	–	mid 2nd c
[b11]	251	–	6-12	NW	yes	–	mid 2nd c
[b12]	255	female	adult	SW	yes	–	mid 2nd c
[b13]*	89	–	adult	–	–	–	mid 2nd c
[b14]	56	–	adolescent	NNW	?	–	mid 2nd c
[b15]	107/108	–	0-5	?	yes	–	mid 2nd c
[b16]	147	female	adult	SW	–	yes	mid 2nd c
[b17]	126	–	adolescent	SW	yes	yes	mid 2nd c
[b18]	58	male	adult	NW	–	yes	?mid 2nd c
[b19]	167	female	17-25	SE	–	yes	mid 2nd c
[b20]	139	–	26-45	NW	–	–	mid 2nd c
[b21]	314	–	adult	SW	?	yes	mid 2nd c
[b22]	325	female	17-25	SE	–	yes	mid 2nd c
[b23]	347	–	neonate	S ?	–	–	mid 2nd c
[b24]*	52	male	adult	–	–	–	mid 2nd c
[b25]	178	male	17-25	NW	yes	yes	late 2nd/3rd c
[b26]	150	–	6-12	SE	yes	yes	late 2nd/3rd c
[b27]	242	female	26-45	SE	yes	–	late 2nd/3rd c
[b28]*	291	–	17-25	–	–	yes	?3rd c
[b29]	123	–	6-12	NE	–	yes	mid 3rd c
[b30]*	48	male	>45	–	–	–	mid 3rd c
* cremation							

Table 6 Summary of cremated human remains

Context	Colour	Weight (kg)	Max size of bone (mm)	Age (yrs)	Sex
38	grey	1.00	36 × 35	adult	female
48	white	1.10	170 × 21	>45	male
52	white	1.58	40 × 20	adult	male
89	grey	0.25	71 × 50	adult	?
291	white	0.50	75 × 15	17-25	?

5

Specialist reports

5.1 The late Roman pottery

Fiona Seeley

The pottery derived from the cemetery area is discussed in the context of the cemetery in section 3.2, above. The vessels which came from the individual features are detailed within the burial catalogue (chapter 4, above). However, a large group of late Roman material was recovered from the late 4th-century infilling of the roadside ditch. It is discussed in its wider context here.

The group, dated to *c* AD 350–400, comprised 176 sherds, 4.45 EVEs (estimated vessel equivalents) (9036g weight). It was subjected to full quantification and illustration to contribute to the ongoing study of late Roman pottery assemblages in London (Symonds & Tomber 1994) – Tables 7–11 of quantified data. (Tables 12–15 list the pottery codes.) Although the group is too small to be a valid statistical sample, it has been compared to other quantified groups of the same date to identify general trends within fabrics and forms present. This group has been illustrated comprehensively (Figs 39 and 40), including residual material such as the Dressel 20 amphora rim <P55> (BAETE 8DR20PW27) which is dated *c* AD 120–80 on its rim form (Peacock & Williams 1986, fig 66, no. 27).

The most commonly occurring fine ware in the assemblage is Oxfordshire Red Colour-coated ware (OXRC) (10.8% sherd count/18.9% EVEs/4.9% weight). The forms for OXRC and other fabrics of the Oxfordshire industries have all been correlated to Young's study of the industry (1977) and his dates have been quoted where appropriate. Several OXRC bowl forms are present in the assemblage, several of which are variants of the necked bowl form C75. The variants illustrated include those with white-painted decoration (Young 1977, fig 62, no. C77) <P32>, and rouletting and stamped decoration (Young 1977, fig 62, nos C78.1–8; fig 63, nos C78.9–19) <P33>. Young suggests that the C77 forms are dated to *c* AD 340–400+. Other bowl forms in OXRC include another vessel <P34> which has rouletted and stamped decoration and is probably one of the many variants of the C81 (Young 1977, fig 64, nos C81–C84; fig 65, nos C84–C86), a form which is generally dated *c* AD 300–400. A 4th-century date is also given to the mortarium form C100 <P35> which also occurs in this group (Young 1977, fig 67, no. C100.2). Other forms in OXRC include two separate examples of a C98 bowl from [412] and [402] but which are not illustrated as they are too abraded. This form is dated by Young to AD 350–400+ (Young 1977, fig 67, no. C98). Other Oxfordshire wares include an Oxford White-slipped ware Young Type WC7 mortarium <P36> and Oxford White ware Young Type M22 mortaria (OXWW 7M22) <P37> <P38>. The other late Romano-British fineware product represented is Nene Valley Colour-coated ware (NVCC). The base <P39> is slipped internally and externally and has a defined foot-ring. There is a carination where the foot meets the body of the vessel. The other vessel <P40> is either a dish

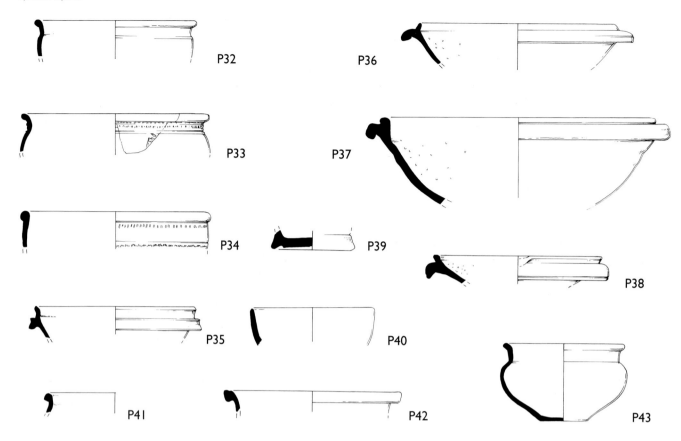

Fig 39 *Late Roman pottery vessels <P32> – <P43> recovered from the Period 4 roadside ditch Group 10 (scale 1:4)*

<P32> [180] OXRC 4N WPD
<P33> [331] OXRC 4N ROD STD
<P34> [202] OXRC 4 ROD STD
<P35> [412] OXRC 7C100
<P36> [202] OXWC 7WC7
<P37> [331] OXWW 7M22
<P38> [402] OXWW 7M22
<P39> [202] NVCC base
<P40> [412] NVCC 4/5
<P41> [331] PORD 2T
<P42> [202] VRW 2T
<P43> [402] SAND 2

or a bowl. It is most likely to be a simple-rim dish (5J) as the interior of the vessel shows it to be curving inwards to form a base similar to one illustrated in Howe *et al* which is dated to the 4th century (1980, 24, fig 7, no. 87). Alternatively it could be a copy of a Drag 38 bowl which are also produced by the industry and dated to the late 3rd and 4th centuries (Howe *et al* 1980, fig 7, no. 83).

One of the most interesting aspects of the assemblage is the amount of grog-tempered fabrics (7.4% sherd count/3.1% EVEs/4% weight) which are possibly contemporary with the rest of the group. Two grog-tempered vessels are illustrated: a bowl and the base of a jar. The bowl <P44> is in a hard-fired reduced light grey fabric. The fabric contains large light grey grog in a silty matrix with occasional ill-sorted quartz and moderate small black inclusions. The jar <P45> is handmade and in a dark grey fabric with a silty matrix containing

frequent large angular grey grog, occasional ill-sorted quartz and occasional ?burnt-out inclusions. Similar fabrics have been found elsewhere in the ditch including a further base in [116]. It is suggested that as there is little residuality within the group as a whole – and given that the GROG sherds are not abraded, are of a good size, have sherd links and that a complete profile of the bowl remains – these fabrics are probably contemporary with the rest of the assemblage rather than being residual.

Oxidised wares include a Portchester 'D' ware necked jar (PORD 2T) <P41> and a Verulamium Region White ware necked jar (VRW 2T) <P42>. The VRW jar is slightly lid-seated. Although the presence of VRW is undoubtedly residual in this assemblage, it has been noted from recent extensive spot-dating on backlog sites from Southwark that the VRW type of form that tends to be most commonly found in later groups is the jar.

Alice Holt Farnham ware (AHFA) is the most commonly occurring fabric by sherd count and EVEs (27.%/43.6%). The group has a good range of forms typical of the late Alice Holt industry, most of which can be paralleled with products from the kiln site (Lyne & Jefferies 1979). The AHFA later everted-rim jar (2FX) <P46> has an applied dark grey/black slip on the neck, shoulder and the interior of the rim. Evidence from the kiln site suggests that the introduction of this technique of slipping parts of vessels rather than just burnishing starts occurring in the late 3rd century (Lyne & Jefferies 1979, 35). The large storage jar (2V) <P48> despite being abraded also has black slip still visible on the rim; this form is dated to c AD 350–420 at the kiln site (Lyne & Jefferies 1979, fig 25, 1C.6). The other illustrated jar has a narrower neck and combed decoration (2U COMB) <P47> and is given dates of AD 300–420 (Lyne & Jefferies 1979, fig 23, 1A.16). The most commonly occurring type of bowl is the flanged bowl (4M) particularly in AHFA; three examples are illustrated to show the variety in rim forms. Two of these vessels have short stubby flanges, <P50> and <P51>, which are typical of late 4th-century assemblages in the City (Symonds & Tomber 1994, 76). The third bowl <P52> differs in having a hooked flange and black/dark grey slip on the rim. A further flanged bowl occurs in Black-burnished-type 1 ware (BB1) <P53>. The flange is not as substantial and stubby as the examples in AHFA and it is decorated with burnished intersecting arcs (ARCX). Plain-rim dishes (5J) occur in both BB1 and AHFA.

The BB1 example <P54> is shallow and decorated with burnished intersecting arcs. The AHFA dish <P49> has two grooves below the rim and is burnished externally and internally. It is straight-sided and does not curve inwards at the top. A similar vessel is illustrated from the kiln site although unlike the Great Dover Street example it is also decorated (Lyne & Jefferies 1979, 48, fig 36, no. 6A.12).

There were very few vessel links between the contexts despite the reoccurrence of the same fabrics and forms appearing in several of them. This may be partly due to the level of abraded surfaces and edges (which is a common feature of most of the pottery from this site). But multiples of the same form are occurring in the ditch and are not the same vessel such as the three examples of 7M22. Also several sherds from OXRC rouletted bowls occur in the same context

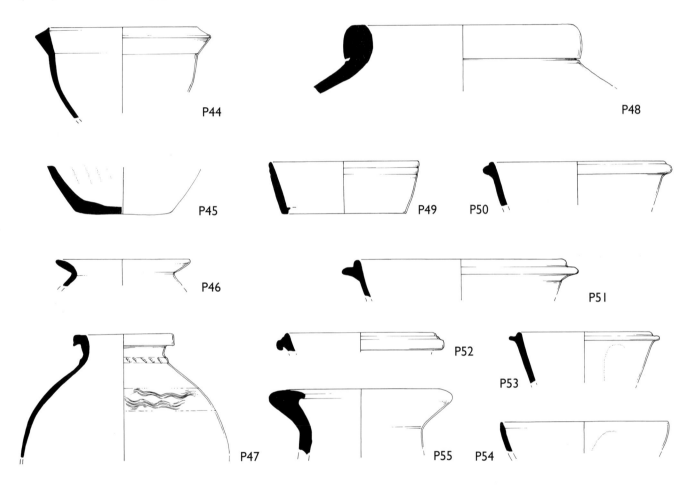

Fig 40 Late Roman pottery vessels <P44> – <P55> recovered from the Period 4 roadside ditch Group 10 (scale 1:4)

<P44> [180] GROG 4
<P45> [402] GROG 2
<P46> [412] AHFA 2FX
<P47> [402] AHFA 2U COMB
<P48> [116] AHFA 2V
<P49> [402] AHFA 5J
<P50> [135] AHFA 4M
<P51> [116] AHFA 4M
<P52> [412] AHFA 4M
<P53> [402] BB1 4M ARCX
<P54> [412] BB1 5J ARCX
<P55> [180] BAETE 8DR20PW27

but are all from different vessels. In addition to this there are several complete NVCC bases representing numerous individual vessels. There were no complete vessels and few profiles within the group.

The general trends within the assemblage confirm those seen in the late group from Billingsgate bath-house (Symonds & Tomber 1994, 77–80) which is dated c AD 350–450. These trends are: a high percentage of wares from the Oxfordshire industry (15.4% sherd count/34.8%EVEs/13.5%weight) and a variety of fabrics and forms from within that industry; the

Table 7 Late Roman pottery – raw data by fabric

Fabric	Rows	% Rows	Sherd count	% Sherd count	EVEs	% EVEs	Weight (g)	% Weight
AHFA	22	22.2	48	27.3	1.94	43.6	1619	17.9
AMPH	1	1.0	1	0.6	0	0.0	62	0.7
AMPH1	1	1.0	1	0.6	0	0.0	26	0.3
BAET	3	3.0	11	6.3	0	0.0	1500	16.6
BAETE	2	2.0	9	5.1	0.13	2.9	2725	30.2
BAETL	2	2.0	2	1.1	0	0.0	205	2.3
BB1	4	4.0	4	2.3	0.18	4.0	76	0.8
BBS	2	2.0	2	1.1	0	0.0	48	0.5
BHWS	1	1.0	1	0.6	0	0.0	27	0.3
COAR	1	1.0	2	1.1	0	0.0	23	0.3
FINE	1	1.0	1	0.6	0	0.0	18	0.2
GAUL	2	2.0	2	1.1	0	0.0	15	0.2
GAUL1	2	2.0	2	1.1	0	0.0	18	0.2
GROG	6	6.1	13	7.4	0.14	3.1	357	4.0
NKSH	1	1.0	1	0.6	0	0.0	27	0.3
NVCC	6	6.1	7	4	0.16	3.6	243	2.7
OXID	3	3.0	6	3.4	0	0.0	105	1.2
OXRC	17	17.2	19	10.8	0.84	18.9	441	4.9
OXWC	1	1.0	1	0.6	0.13	2.9	65	0.7
OXWS	1	1.0	1	0.6	0	0.0	42	0.5
OXWW	4	4.0	6	3.4	0.58	13.0	667	7.4
PORD	4	4.0	4	2.3	0.1	2.2	184	2.0
RWS	1	1.0	1	0.6	0	0.0	21	0.2
SAMCG	1	1.0	1	0.6	0.05	1.1	5	0.1
SAND	8	8.1	26	14.8	0.12	2.7	457	5.1
VRW	2	2.0	4	2.3	0.08	1.8	60	0.7
Totals	**99**	**100.0**	**176**	**100.0**	**4.45**	**100.0**	**9036**	**100.0**

Rows On the Oracle database, each line (row) consisting of a unique fabric, form and decoration combination.

Table 8 Late Roman pottery – raw data by form

Form	Rows	% Rows	Sherd count	% Sherd count	EVEs	% EVEs	Weight (g)	% Weight
unknown	26	26.3	44	25	0	0.0	674	7.5
2	12	12.1	34	19.3	0.12	2.7	727	8.0
2/3	1	1.0	1	0.6	0	0.0	32	0.4
2FX	1	1.0	1	0.6	0.18	4.0	42	0.5
2T	2	2.0	2	1.1	0.18	4.0	27	0.3
2U	1	1.0	8	4.5	1	22.5	305	3.4
2V	7	7.1	12	6.8	0.15	3.4	680	7.5
3	3	3.0	8	4.5	0	0.0	157	1.7
4	7	7.1	9	5.1	0.3	6.7	232	2.6
4/5	4	4.0	5	2.8	0.16	3.6	269	3.0
4DR38	1	1.0	1	0.6	0	0.0	32	0.4
4M	5	5.1	5	2.8	0.59	13.3	279	3.1
4N	3	3.0	3	1.7	0.33	7.4	48	0.5
5	1	1.0	1	0.6	0.05	1.1	5	0.1
5J	2	2.0	2	1.1	0.2	4.5	66	0.7
7	2	2.0	2	1.1	0	0.0	52	0.6
7C100	1	1.0	1	0.6	0.18	4.0	48	0.5
7C97	1	1.0	1	0.6	0	0.0	25	0.3
7C98	2	2.0	2	1.1	0.17	3.8	63	0.7
7M22	3	3.0	5	2.8	0.58	13.0	657	7.3
7WC7	1	1.0	1	0.6	0.13	2.9	65	0.7
8	6	6.1	6	3.4	0	0.0	174	1.9
8DR20	5	5.1	20	11.4	0	0.0	4239	46.9
8DR20PW27	1	1.0	1	0.6	0.13	2.9	130	1.4
8G	1	1.0	1	0.6	0	0.0	8	0.1
Totals	**99**	**100.0**	**176**	**100**	**4.45**	**100.0**	**9036**	**100.0**

dominance of AHFA compared to BB1 as the main reduced ware; the main bowl form being the 4M with those examples with a short stubby flange being the most common; and the dominance of the AHFA large storage jar. However, it is noticeable that there is no Much Hadham ware (MHAD) or Calcite-gritted ware (CALC) in the assemblage, two fabrics which appear in significant quantities in the Billingsgate group. This group, albeit small, exhibits many of the main trends

Table 9 Late Roman pottery – raw data by ware

Ware	Rows	% Rows	Sherd count	% Sherd count	EVEs	% EVEs	Weight (g)	% Weight
AMPH	13	13.1	28	15.9	0.13	2.9	4551	50.4
BBTP	6	6.1	6	3.4	0.18	4.0	124	1.4
FNRB	24	24.2	27	15.3	1.13	25.4	749	8.3
FNRD	1	1.0	1	0.6	0	0.0	18	0.2
OXID	16	16.2	23	13.1	0.76	17.1	1106	12.2
REDU	30	30.3	74	42.0	2.06	46.3	2076	23.0
SAM	1	1.0	1	0.6	0.05	1.1	5	0.1
TEMP	8	8.1	16	9.1	0.14	3.1	407	4.5
Totals	**99**	**100.0**	**176**	**100.0**	**4.45**	**100.0**	**9036**	**100.0**

Table 10 Late Roman pottery – raw data by type

Type	Rows	% Rows	Sherd count	% Sherd count	EVEs	% EVEs	Weight (g)	% Weight
unknown	26	26.3	44	25	0	0.0	674	7.5
amphora	13	13.1	28	15.9	0.13	2.9	4551	50.4
beaker	3	3.0	8	4.5	0	0.0	157	1.7
bowl	16	16.2	18	10.2	1.22	27.4	591	6.5
bowl/dish	4	4.0	5	2.8	0.16	3.6	269	3.0
dish	3	3.0	3	1.7	0.25	5.6	71	0.8
jar	24	24.2	58	33.0	1.63	36.6	1813	20.1
mortarium	10	10.1	12	6.8	1.06	23.8	910	10.1
Totals	**99**	**100.0**	**176**	**100**	**4.45**	**100.0**	**9036**	**100.0**

Table 11 Late Roman pottery – raw data by source

Source	Rows	% Rows	Sherd count	% Sherd count	EVEs	% EVEs	Weight (g)	% Weight
Britain	85	85.9	147	83.5	4.27	96.0	4480	49.6
Central Gaul	1	1.0	1	0.6	0.05	1.1	5	0.1
South-east Gaul	4	4.0	4	2.3	0	0.0	33	0.4
Spain	7	7.1	22	12.5	0.13	2.9	4430	49.0
unknown	2	2.0	2	1.1	0	0.0	88	1.0
Totals	**99**	**100.0**	**176**	**100.0**	**4.45**	**100.0**	**9036**	**100.0**

seen in late 4th-century Roman pottery assemblages in London and is further evidence for late Roman activity in this area of Southwark.

5.2 Building materials

Susan Pringle

The building materials were quantified by fabric, form and context using the standard Museum of London recording sheet and fabric codes. The fabrics which are referred to in the text below are listed at the end of this section, and samples are held at the Museum of London. The data were computerised to facilitate the correlation of the building materials with the stratigraphic periods, and to assist with the interpretation of the archaeological features. The results of this analysis have been integrated as far as possible with the main body of the report.

The majority of the ceramic building material found in London is made with clays containing varying amounts of quartz, which fire to various shades of red. Most tile from Southwark is in the same fabric types as those used in other areas of London, which means that it probably came from the same kilns. In the early Roman period, large quantities of tile were produced from local sources, but there appears from the mid 2nd century on to be an increasing reuse of tile from earlier buildings, accompanied by the appearance of new types of non-local tiles. By the 4th century it seems probable that most of the tile and brick used in building construction in London was reused material, supplemented by small amounts of non-local products.

Brick and tile

The brick and tile from the site is mostly early Roman and reflects the material in use in Southwark in the 1st and early 2nd centuries. Most of the materials were probably reused before eventual disposal. Some contexts, particularly the later

Table 12 Roman pottery fabric codes

Code	Description
Amphorae	
AMPH	Miscellaneous amphora fabric type
AMPH 1-7	Amphorae
BAET	Baetican Dressel 20 amphora fabric, unspecified
BAETE	Baetican Dressel 20/Haltern 70 amphora fabric, early
BAETL	Baetican Dressel 20 amphora fabric, late
CADIZ	Camulodunum type 186 amphora fabric
GAUL	Miscellaneous Gaulish amphora fabric
GAUL 1	Pélichet 47/Dressel 30 amphora fabric
ITFEL	Italian feldspathic Dressel 2-4 amphora fabric
Samian wares	
SAMCG	Central Gaulish samian ware
SAMEG	East Gaulish samian ware
SAMLG	La Graufesenque samian ware
SAMMV	Les Martres de Veyre samian ware
Imported fine wares	
CCIMP	Miscellaneous imported colour-coated ware
CGWH	Central Gaulish Colour-coated ware white fabric
KOLN	Cologne Colour-coated ware
LYON	Lyon Colour-coated ware
MOSL	Moselkeramik
Romano-British fine wares	
LOMA	London Marbled
NVCC	Nene Valley Colour-coated ware
OXRC	Oxfordshire Red/Brown Colour-coated ware
OXWC	Oxfordshire White Colour-coated ware
Black-burnished-type wares	
BB1	Black-burnished 1 ware
BB2	Black-burnished 2 ware
BB2F	Black-burnished 2 ware with fine fabric
BBS	Black-burnished-style ware
TSK	Thameside Kent ware
Fine reduced wares	
FINE	Miscellaneous fine ware
FMIC	Fine Micaceous Black/Grey ware
Reduced wares	
AHBB	Alice Holt Black-burnished-type ware
AHFA	Alice Holt/Farnham ware
AHSU	Alice Holt/Surrey ware
ERSB	Early Roman Sandy ware, B
HWC	Highgate 'C' Sand-tempered ware
SAND	Miscellaneous sand-tempered ware
VRG	Verulamium Region Grey ware
Tempered wares	
COAR	Miscellaneous coarse ware
GROG	Grog-tempered ware
HWB	Highgate 'B' Grog-tempered ware
NKSH	North Kent Shell-tempered ware
Oxidised wares	
BHWS	Brockley Hill White slip
COLWW	Colchester White ware
HOO	Hoo ware
LOXI	Local Oxidised ware
NFSE	North French/South-east English Oxidised ware
OXID	Miscellaneous oxidised ware
OXWS	Oxfordshire White-slipped Red ware
OXWW	Oxfordshire White ware
PORD	Portchester 'D' ware
RWS	Miscellaneous red- and white-slipped ware
VCWS	Verulamium Region Coarse White-slipped ware
VRR	Verulamium Region Red ware
VRW	Verulamium Region White ware
Miscellaneous wares	
CC	Miscellaneous colour-coated wares

Table 13 Roman pottery form codes

Code	Description
1	Miscellaneous or otherwise unidentifiable flagon
1B7	Cup-mouthed ring-necked flagon
1B7-9	Cup-mouthed ring-necked flagon
1C	Pinch-mouthed flagon
1DX	Later disc-mouthed flagon
1H	Flagon with continuous body
2	Miscellaneous or otherwise unidentifiable jar
2/3	Jar or beaker; enclosed vessel
2A	Bead-rim jar
2A1-4	Bead-rim jar: simple thickening, triangular section
2A15	Finely moulded bead-rim jar with grooves beneath rim
2A17	Black-burnished-type bead-rim jar
2AX	Later bead-rim jar
2C	Necked jar with carinated shoulder; 'figure 7' rim
2E	Round-bodied necked jar with burnished shoulder
2F	Black-burnished-type everted-rim jar
2FX	Late AHFA version of 2F
2K	Two-handled 'honey pot' jar
2T	Otherwise undistinguishable necked jar
2U	Narrow-necked globular jar
2V	Storage jar
3	Miscellaneous or otherwise unidentifiable beaker
3B	Ovoid beaker
3DE72	Déchelette form 72 beaker
3F	'Poppyhead' beaker
3J	Bag-shaped beaker
3K	Necked globular beaker
4	Miscellaneous or otherwise unidentifiable bowl
4/5	Bowl/dish
4D	Wide bowl with carination & mouldings; imitation 4DR29
4DR30	Dragendorff form 30 bowl
4DR37	Dragendorff form 37 bowl
4DR38	Dragendorff form 38 bowl
4G226	Bowl with incipient flange (Gillam form 226)
4H	Rounded-rim Black-burnished-type bowl
4M	Black-burnished-type flanged bowl
4N	Necked bowl
4RT12	Ritterling form 12 bowl
5	Miscellaneous or otherwise unidentifiable plate
5A	Plate with plain exterior profile
5DR15/17	Dragendorff form 15/17 dish
5DR18	Dragendorff form 18 dish
5DR35/36	Dragendorff form 35/36 dish
5DR36	Dragendorff form 36 dish
5J	Dish with simple rim
6	Miscellaneous or otherwise unidentifiable cup
6DR27	Dragendorff form 27 cup
6DR33	Dragendorff form 33 cup
7	Miscellaneous or otherwise unidentifiable mortarium
7C100	Young type C100 mortarium
7C97	Young type C97 mortarium
7C98	Young type C98 mortarium; as C97 with white-painted decoration
7EWAL	Early wall-sided mortarium
7HOF	Hooked-flange mortarium
7M22	Young type M22 mortarium
7WC7	Oxford white-slipped mortarium copying Young type M22
8	Miscellaneous amphorae
8C184	Rhodian-type amphora
8DR20	Dressel form 20 amphora
8DR20PW11	Dressel form 20 amphora
8DR20PW17	Dressel form 20 amphora
8DR20PW27	Dressel form 20 amphora
8DR20PW30	Dressel form 20 amphora
8G	Pélichet 47/Dressel form 30/Gauloise-type amphora
8G4	Gauloise type 4 amphora
9A	Lid (usually post-70)
9C	Tazza
9F	Tettina/feeding bottle
9LA	Lamp

Table 14 Roman pottery decoration codes

Code	Description
AL	Black-burnished-type acute-lattice decoration
ARCS	Intersecting arcs
ARCX	Arcs on later Black-burnished ware forms
BDD	Barbotine dot decoration
BUD	Burnished decoration
COMB	Combed decoration
CR	Cornice rim
END	Elongated indentations
NCD	Incised decoration
OAL	Open acute-lattice decoration
OL	Obtuse-lattice decoration
RCD1	Sand/quartz roughcast decoration
RCD2	Clay pellet/grog roughcast decoration
ROD	Rouletted decoration
STD	Stamped decoration
UND	Unidentifiable indentations
WL	Wavy line decoration
WPD	White paint decoration

Table 15 Roman pottery ware codes

AMPH	Amphorae
BBTP	Black-burnished-type wares
FNRB	Romano-British fine wares
FNRD	Fine reduced wares
OXID	Oxidised wares
REDU	Reduced wares
SAM	Samian wares
TEMP	Tempered wares

roadside ditch fills, contain later tile, but there is no sign of new tile being brought in for the construction of the earlier monuments.

There is, however, tentative evidence of a 'tileworking' horizon in Period 3 (c AD 120–250). The tile flakes may have derived from the construction or destruction of roofs or other features which incorporated tile. Tileworking flakes were recovered mainly from burials [b10] to [b12] in walled cemetery Structure 3 and burials [b15] and [b28] in Open Area 4. They also occurred in small quantities in burial [b8] in walled cemetery Structure 1. Their retrieval here probably owed a lot to the care with which the graves were excavated, but they also occurred in non-burial contexts. The majority of flakes are in fabric 2454, which is generally thought to have been first in use in London between c AD 50 and AD 70/80. As the features from which the tile flakes were recovered were dated to between AD 100–40 by pottery, it is likely that the tile flakes were residual or that any tile being worked on site was reused from an earlier building – conceivably either Building 1, the piled building, or Building 2, the possible temple. The possibility of material being brought in from another source cannot be ruled out. Structure 1 has flakes in the local red fabric only; this could indicate that Structures 1 and 3 were not constructed (or refurbished) at the same time. If this is the case, the distribution of flakes of white tile might

suggest that Structure 3 is slightly later than Structure 1.

Aside from use as roofing and in the construction of walls, tile was also sometimes used for decorative detailing and for smaller mortar and rubble structures within the walled cemeteries. These would probably have been faced with stone, stucco or mortar.

Painted plaster and *opus signinum* mortar

All the plaster fragments recorded are of similar type, consisting of a layer of distinctive gritty, fairly fine, orange *opus signinum* covered with a layer of white *opus signinum* containing fairly coarse tile fragments. The usual thickness is between 2.5mm and 4mm. The white layer has been smoothed and painted with red ochre, without the usual addition of a layer of fine white plaster skim or *intonaco*. There is no sign of decoration on the red-painted surfaces, or of any other colour schemes.

The *opus signinum* is associated mainly with walled cemetery Structure 3 although some also occurs in Open Areas 2 and 4. None was recorded from the possible temple, Building 2, or the backfill of its attached masonry well, nor was there any recorded from walled cemetery Structure 1, or the possible mausoleum, Structure 2.

As *opus signinum* floors are generally much thicker than this material, it is likely to have been wall render. Two fragments, from the post-Roman sequence [137] and [202], appear to be from right-angled corners, and are probably facings from a mortar and rubble structure. That from [202] has a flake of Reigate stone preserved in the angle; it presumably formed part of the flat, smooth, red-painted rendering of a structure which incorporated Reigate stone blocks. A brick with traces of similar red-skimmed *opus signinum* came from the fill of the roadside ditch in Open Area 2.

Building stone

The major building stone found on the site was Kentish ragstone. This was used in the construction of walls for Building 2, and Structures 1 and 2. The walls of Structure 3, although robbed, appear to have been constructed using mortared flint as was the central plinth. Some knapped flint was recovered from a nearby post-medieval pit.

The Reigate stone from the site was associated mainly with Building 2, and Structures 1 and 2, with a small amount from burial [b26] in Open Area 4. Reigate stone, which was quarried in Surrey at Reigate and Merstham, was only very rarely used in the City in the Roman period and its use here is of special interest. It has also been found in Southwark in association with pre-Boudican buildings in Borough High Street (Drummond-Murray & Thompson in prep). As none was recorded from Structure 3, it is possible that Structures 1 and 2 incorporated Reigate stone rubble from the destruction of Building 2, material which may not have been available when Structure 3 was built. If so, this would support the interpretation of the tileworking evidence to indicate that

Structure 1 was built before Structure 3.

A fragment of calcareous tufa with what appears to be a cut face came from the timber well in Open Area 4. This is likely to have been used to form a vaulted ceiling in one of the funerary structures; it most probably came from the possible mausoleum, Structure 2.

Very little decorative stone was noted. A fragment of Purbeck marble slab 33mm thick was recorded from the later roadside ditch fills. This was associated with some of the distinctive orange *opus signinum*, and both are likely to have come from the cemetery. It could have been used for flooring, or as veneer inside one of the structures. The only other stone which may have been in use was some abraded fine-grained sandstone from burial [b28]. One 15mm thick slab had mortar on the sides and base, and was probably used for flooring.

Ceramic building material fabrics

Fabric descriptions have been described with the aid of a binocular microscope (x10 magnification). The following conventions are used in the descriptions. The terminology for the frequency of inclusions is as follows: sparse, moderate, common, abundant. Where grain sizes are not specified, average sizes of sand-sized inclusions (up to 2mm) are defined as follows: very fine, up to 0.1mm; fine, 0.1–0.25mm; medium 0.25–0.5mm; coarse, 0.5–1mm; very coarse, larger than 1mm.

1 Fabric group 2815 (2452, 2459, 3004, 3006)

These tiles, which all have red fabrics, come from a number of kilns situated along Watling Street between London and St Albans, within 30km of London. As the tileries used very similar clays, it is not usually possible to attribute the tiles which comprise fabric group 2815 to specific kiln sites.

Fabric 2452: a fine fabric with sparse to moderate quartz (up to 0.5mm). Usually with sparse calcium carbonate and iron oxide (up to 2mm).

Fabric 2459: a fine, sandy fabric with a scatter of quartz grains above 0.2mm in size. Sparse calcium carbonate and iron oxide (up to 1mm). Tiles in this fabric with very fine moulding sand (2459B) are later in date than those with normal moulding sand (2459A). A rarer late version has straw moulding (2459C).

Fabric 3004: a sandy fabric with common to abundant, coarse to very coarse quartz grains (up to 0.7mm) and sparse iron oxide and calcium carbonate (up to 0.7mm).

Fabric 3006: a fine, slightly sandy fabric with moderate to common coarse quartz (up to 0.3mm), with occasional iron oxide and calcium carbonate.

Fabrics 2452, 2459A, 3004 and 3006 are probably not made after *c* AD 160, being replaced by tiles in related fabrics 2459B and 2459C from *c* AD 140 on.

2 Fabric 2454

The second important source of tile in the earliest period was probably the tilery situated in the Eccles area of north-west Kent, on the Medway. This produced the distinctive yellow and white tiles, which are found on all sites in Southwark. They seem not to be imported into London after the early Flavian period, *c* AD 70–80.

Fabric 2454: a distinctive yellow, pink or yellowish-white fabric, usually well fired, with moderate to common colourless or 'rose' quartz (most up to 0.5mm), and sparse to medium iron oxide and calcium carbonate inclusions (up to 2mm). Some examples have red moulding sand.

3 Fabric group 3023, 3060

These fabrics, the products from the tile kiln at Radlett in Hertfordshire, are made from a distinctive clay. They are present, usually in smaller quantities than the 2815 group and the Eccles products, in the pre-Boudican period, and seem to go out of production in the early to mid 2nd century.

Fabric 3060: red, orange or brown fabric with abundant fine quartz (up to 0.3mm), with common very fine black iron oxides (up to 0.1mm), and scatter of very coarse red iron oxides (up to 2mm).

Fabric 3023: similar to fabric 3060, but with cream silty inclusions (up to 6mm).

4 Fabric 3050

One of the distinctive groups of tiles occurring in the late Roman period in Southwark is of tiles with varying amounts of dark-coloured quartz, manufactured at kilns at Reigate in Surrey. The date range is *c* AD 120/140 to the early 3rd century or a little later.

Fabric 3050: usually highly fired with varying amounts (from sparse to common) of fine to medium, dark red 'rose' quartz (up to 0.3mm), with varying amounts of coarse colourless quartz (up to 0.8mm), sparse iron oxides and calcium carbonate. The clay matrix may have silty streaks and bands, or cream mottling.

5 Fabric group 2453 (fabrics 2453, 2457)

These distinctive calcareous tiles are widely distributed along the coast of southern and south-east England, but the location of the tilery or tileries supplying Southwark has still to be established. Dates: mid/late 2nd to end of 3rd century. Tiles in this group of fabrics often have dark red moulding sand.

Fabric 2453: usually pink in colour, but cream, yellow or brown examples occur. Common very coarse inclusions of yellowish-white clay (up to 6mm) in often mottled clay matrix. Sparse iron oxide (up to 1mm). Some have common coarse quartz (up to 0.8mm).

Fabric 2457: light grey or greyish-brown fabric with abundant calcium carbonate and fine grey shell fragments with scatter of fine quartz (up to 0.2mm) in background clay matrix. Moderate coarse grey or white shell fragments (up to 6mm), coarse quartz (up to 0.8mm) and iron oxide inclusions (up to 0.8mm).

6 Individual fabrics

Fabric 3005: pink, light orange or cream matrix, usually mottled and containing bands or lenses of clay, with very fine background quartz. Sparse to common inclusions of medium, colourless or rose, quartz and coarse red and yellowish-white fragments of clay or silt (up to 5mm). Source unknown. Dates: c AD 125–230.

Fabric 3019: light brownish-orange, sometimes with light grey core. Common blocky siltstone inclusions (up to 7mm) and red iron oxide (up to 4mm). Scatter of quartz (up to 0.3mm) and occasional calcium carbonate. Commonly a brick fabric. The source is probably Hampshire, possibly the kilns at Braxells Farm, near Southampton or at Little London, near Silchester. This fabric is dated to AD 100–20+ in the City, although roof tile in this fabric occurs in Southwark in the 1st century. It is possible that this early roof tile may come from different kilns to the 2nd-century brick production.

Fabric 3028: orange with common, well-sorted, medium quartz (up to 0.4mm), sparse to common rounded silty inclusions (up to 6mm) and red iron oxide (up to 1mm). Some examples have bands of light-coloured silty clay. One of a group of fabrics which are characterised by the presence of cream, yellow or white silty inclusions in an orange or light orange clay matrix. Their most likely source is the Weald area south of London, although they may come from more than one kiln site. Source unknown. Dated AD 70–100/120.

Fabric 3051: pink, orange or yellow mottled matrix with cream lensing. Common, poorly sorted, colourless or rose quartz (up to 0.4mm), moderate rounded iron oxide (up to 1.2mm), occasional calcium carbonate inclusions (up to 1.4mm) and larger rock fragments (up to 5mm). Commonly a brick fabric. Source unknown. Date: AD 50/70–80/120.

Fabric 3070: orange fabric with abundant inclusions of very coarse quartz (up to 1mm) and numerous very fine (less than 0.05mm) black iron oxides. Sparse, very coarse inclusions of dark red iron

oxide (up to 0.8mm). Coarser sandy texture than 3004. Rare. Source uncertain, but possibly from one of the kilns making tiles in fabric group 2815. Date: AD 55–80.

5.3 Sculptures and architectural fragments

T F C Blagg

<A1> Head of a bearded god, possibly a water deity

<1> [335] (Fig 41)
Height 255mm. Width 143mm
Fine-textured oolitic limestone, possibly Bath stone or an associated stone from the Cotswold region
The head is carved in the round and broken at the neck. Most of the nose has been broken off and the left side of the head has been more exposed to weathering. The proportions of the face are more elongated than is natural. The eye sockets are

Fig 41 *Roman carved stone head <A1>, possibly a river god, probably from a funerary structure and found in the roadside ditch outside Structure 1*

deeply cut and the irises have been indicated by drilling. The nostrils have also been carved with a drill. The lips are prominent, and the ends of the moustache overhang the recesses at the sides of the mouth. The beard is cut quite close to the profile of the chin. The lobe and edge of the right ear are clearly defined, but most of the left ear has been abraded away. The hair of the head is carved in thick locks swept back from the forehead, straight on top but more wavy at the back and where they hang down behind the nape of the neck. The channels which define the locks have been cut with a chisel but no other tool marks are visible. The technique of the carving, in particular the use of the drill and the depth of carving of the hair and facial features, would indicate a 2nd-century or later date.

The beard and luxuriant hair have obvious parallels with representations of water deities: notably the marble head and bust from the Walbrook Mithraeum (Toynbee 1986, 25–7; Shepherd 1998, 171–2), the relief of a reclining Neptune with three nymphs, probably from Housesteads, and the river god from Chesters, whose beard is bushier however (Coulston & Phillips 1988, 88–9). The closest British parallel is with a reclining Neptune or river god from Cirencester, also carved on oolitic limestone (Henig 1993, 30). Nevertheless, the elongated proportions, deeply cut eye sockets and projecting lips resemble features of some representations of Pan, for example a late Hellenistic marble head from Cyrene (*LIMC* 1997, II, pl 619: Pan 81), and of Silenus, for example a bronze statuette from the House of the Faun, Pompeii (*LIMC* 1997, II, pl 783: Silenoi 233). Both Pan and Silenus feature among Dionysiac imagery in a funerary context (Turcan 1966), and such a water deity as Oceanus, Neptune or even Tamesis, connected with the idea of the journey to the Isles of the Blessed, would be equally appropriate to such a context. The head may therefore be considered as having formed part of a group of sculpture decorating a funerary monument.

<A2> Pine-cone finial

<100> [320] (Fig 42)
Height 230mm. Maximum diameter 207mm
Fine-grained limestone, possibly Caen stone or an associated stone from northern France
The stone is carved with 10 spiral rows of scales, each scale carved with faceted sides and a square convex upper surface. The cone is broken irregularly at the base, where part of a flared projection survives. The uppermost scales are also broken off. In the top a rectangular socket measuring 12mm x 15mm survives to a depth of 44mm. Such a feature is observable on other carved pine cones, such as one from York (Rinaldi Tufi 1983, 54, no. 88), and was presumably intended to contain a metal spike. The scales were carved with a flat chisel, though most of its marks have been smoothed away with a rasp or abrasive. Continuous spiral grooves have been cut ascending from lower left to upper right. Within each spiral the scales have not been defined simply by a second set of continuous spirals intersecting with the first, as on some examples from

Fig 42 Roman carved stone pine-cone finial <A2>, probably originally from a funerary monument and found near the amphora <P29> in Structure 1 (see Fig 14)

other sites, but have been individually carved so that the scales in adjacent rows are staggered at irregular intervals.

Pine cones were carved to decorate funerary monuments, but in Britain this practice has so far been confined to military sites in northern England, Wales and Scotland. This is the first example from the south of the province, and it may have decorated the funeral monument of one of the military personnel present in the capital. Given the identification of a French source for the stone, and the fact that the technique of carving differs from other British examples, it is possible that the piece was imported ready-worked.

<A3> Cornice moulding

<106> [320] (Fig 43)
Height 170mm. Maximum dimensions in plan 530mm x 365mm
Oolitic limestone
The block is carved with mouldings on two adjacent sides. A third side is dressed flat and the fourth side is broken, as are the top and the bottom. Concretion has formed on the surfaces. The main mouldings of the profile are two cyma rectas, the lower being rather more boldly cut. There is the beginning of another cyma recta or a cavetto just above the break at the bottom. It was found in the same context as the pine-cone finial, <A2> above.

Fig 43 *Roman moulded stone cornice <A3> (with profile, scale 1:8), found near the amphora and pine cone in Structure 1 (see Fig 14)*

<A4> Cornice moulding

<105> [335] (Fig 44)
Height 140mm. Maximum dimensions in plan 290mm x
180mm
Oolitic limestone
The block is carved with mouldings on two adjacent sides.
A third side is fairly flat but does not appear to have been

Fig 44 *Roman moulded stone cornice <A4> (with profile, scale 1:8), found in the roadside ditch outside Structure 1*

dressed, and the fourth side and the bottom are irregularly
broken. The surviving profile consists of a fascia, a fillet and a
bold cyma recta. The mouldings are larger in proportion than
those of the preceding item and the grain of the limestone is
coarser. It was found in the same context as the head of the
bearded deity, <A1> above.

<A5> Chamfered block

<75> [388] (not illustrated)
335mm x 230mm x 55mm thick
Oolitic limestone
A large flake from a block with a chamfered edge. No tool
marks are visible.

5.4 The human bones

Bill White

Method

Bone was recorded on the MoLAS Oracle database. The
condition of preservation of individual bones as a consequence
of burial practices was noted and efficiency of recovery
calculated by comparing the number of bones recovered with
that expected from the total number of burials. Cremations
were weighed, the colour noted and the bone passed through
sieves of decreasing mesh size in order to isolate identifiable
fragments (McKinley 1984).

The age of any immature individuals was estimated using
dental development and state of epiphyseal fusion (Bass 1995;
Brothwell 1981) and diaphyseal lengths (Sundick 1978;
Hoffman 1979; Ferembach et al 1980; Ubelaker 1984; Powers
1988), and of adults: tooth wear stages (Brothwell 1981),
state of fusion of cranial sutures (Meindl & Lovejoy 1985)
and morphology of the pubic symphysis (Brooks & Suchey
1990). Sex was estimated using skull and pelvic dimorphism
(Phenice 1969; Ferembach et al 1980; Brothwell 1981) and
tooth crown dimensions (Rö sing 1983). Complementary data
for sex estimation were sought metrically (Bass 1995, see
below) but priority was given to the results of examination
of the pelvis because this was regarded as the most reliable

of the available techniques.

Conventional cranial and post-cranial measurements were taken (Bass 1995; Brothwell 1981) and long-bone lengths were employed in the estimation of stature using the regression equations established by Trotter and Gleser (1952; 1958). Non-metric traits were recorded (Berry & Berry 1967; Finnegan 1978) and where appropriate tested in the elucidation of family relationship.

The jaws were examined for non-metric traits, dental hygiene and pathology (Hillson 1986). Information on general pathology was recorded (Ortner & Putschar 1981), as was the evidence for infectious disease (Rogers & Waldron 1989), joint disease (Rogers & Waldron 1995) and epidemiology (Waldron 1994).

Results

The principal findings from the analysis have been reported above in section 3.1 (The cemetery population) and section 4.1 (burial catalogue). Tabulated supporting data are provided in Tables 16 and 17.

5.5 The animal bones

Kevin Rielly

A small quantity of animal bones (about 12kg or 260 fragments) were recovered from 46 Roman contexts (a further four contexts were post-medieval). In almost all cases, those

deposits with animal bones also contained human bone fragments. It can be assumed that the latter bones were redeposited from adjacent grave fills, clearly showing that the great proportion of these deposits had been disturbed. The effect of such disturbance is to greatly reduce the potential information available from the bone assemblage, that is, in terms of the species used and how they were used throughout the occupation period of the site. However, two aspects of the bone assemblage warranted relatively detailed analysis, these being the single example of an animal burial good found at this site, a chicken in burial [b26], (see 4.1 above) and the horse bones. This latter aspect was thought to be of some value due to an obvious comparison with the assemblages recovered from the eastern cemetery of Roman London (Barber & Bowsher 2000), this site providing, as here, an abundance of horse bones. In addition, the majority of these bones are measurable, allowing for a brief analysis of the size/type of horses used in Roman London.

The horse bones from the roadside ditch

Many of the bone-bearing contexts can be generally dated to either the 1st/2nd centuries AD or the 3rd/4th centuries AD and are mainly from the roadside ditch. Each of these two phases produced bone assemblages where about 5% to 10% of the total fragments were identified as horse. These percentages are very unusual for London sites, where percentages closer to 1% are more normal; for example, within the early and late Roman occupation phases at Winchester Palace the proportion of horse bones was less than 0.1% (Rielly in prep). A likely reason for these low percentages is the decline in the consumption of horseflesh following the arrival of the Romans

Table 16 Calculated stature of four adults

Burial no.	Sex	Stature (cm)	Burial no.	Sex	Stature (cm)
[b4]	M	171	[b19]	F	155
[b8]	M	178	[b22]	F	153
ELRC mean	M	169	ELRC mean	F	158

ELRC mean represents the mean figure from the eastern cemetery of Roman London (Conheeney 2000).

Table 17 Summary of some characteristics of the inhumation burials

Burial no.	Non-metric variation	Dental caries	Spine	Joint osteoarthritis	Healed fracture	Other pathology
[b2]	wormian bones	yes		elbow, wrist	rib	
[b4]		yes	'DISH'			
[b8]	tooth rotation		spondylolysis (L5)			
[b12]				ankles		
[b18]			osteoarthritis	elbows		
[b19]			L5 sacralised		rib (x2)	
[b21]						periostitis
[b22]	perforate septa					
[b25]	third-molar absence	yes		fused tarsals		
[b26]						rickets
[b27]		yes	'DISH'	ankle		

(Wilson 1973, 71–2). As the bone dumps found at these sites were almost entirely composed of food waste, it would follow that horse bones are unlikely to be well represented.

An abundance of horse bones would therefore have to be explained in terms of some non-dietary function. It was noticed that similarly large quantities of horse bones were found at the eastern cemetery sites. The question to be asked, therefore, is whether there is a link between the obvious ritual activities at these cemetery sites (including Great Dover Street) and the abundance of horse bones. At the eastern cemetery sites, there were a number of semi-articulated horse remains, which were interpreted as the remains of disturbed, well-rotted carcasses. It was argued that such disturbance, this occurring fairly soon after the carcass was deposited, is unlikely to have taken place if the horse had represented a ritual deposit. The more likely scenario is that these carcasses were crudely deposited, probably without any attempt at burial, and these were then disturbed either through the subsequent use of this area for inhumation and cremation burials, or through the action of dogs. Undoubtedly the various parts of these carcasses suffered repeated disturbance as the area was used and then reused for the cutting of graves, pits and other features. The horse assemblage is certainly represented by a general mix of parts, showing the original presence of whole animals, and mainly by no more than one or two bones per deposit, showing the extent of the disturbance. With the exception of the semi-articulated remains, the Great Dover Street horse assemblage is similar to that described from the eastern cemetery (Rielly 2000). It could be envisaged that these bones are equally the remains of animals which have undergone the same sequence of disturbance events.

In conclusion, the horses from all of these cemetery sites are likely to represent the remains of redeposited/disturbed whole carcasses, which were originally deposited within an available open area situated outside the city/suburbs. There would appear to be no obvious link to the graves cut into the same area. However, it is clear that horses were dumped within the eastern cemetery both prior to and during the use of the cemetery (Rielly 2000). The presence of horse bones throughout the Great Dover Street deposits argues for a similar continuity of deposition. It is possible that the later use of these sites for the deposition of horse carcasses coincided with a temporary hiatus in the use of the relevant area for burial purposes.

Size

All the horse bones recovered from Great Dover Street were from adult individuals. A large proportion of these were measurable, including two whole metacarpals. The lateral lengths (all measurements following von den Driesch 1976) of these bones were 204.2mm and 194.2mm, from which were calculated shoulder heights of 130.8cm (12.2 hands) and 124.5cm (12.9 hands) respectively (using indices described in von den Driesch & Boessneck 1974). Other measurements tended to complement the size range shown by

these two withers heights (achieved by comparing various dimensions with a skeleton representing an animal of known size within the MoLAS animal bone reference collection), with the exception of a large distal tibia with a distal breadth of 75mm. This may have belonged to an animal about 145cm (14.2 hands) at the shoulder. The smaller range of animals is well within the range of horse sizes found at London sites, while the larger horse is very much at the uppermost part of this range (Rackham 1995, 170). Essentially the horses represented can be described as approximately medium- to large-sized ponies. Both of the metacarpals are fairly stout bones, which could indicate that these animals were used for pulling or carrying, rather than for riding purposes.

5.6 The plant remains – a summary

John Giorgi

Seventy litres of soil from the fill [38] of a *bustum* pit were processed by flotation; the flot was scanned using a binocular microscope while the residues were scanned by eye. Both the flot and residue contained a wide range of charred plant remains together with other biological and artefactual debris. A full description of the plant remains can be found along with a discussion of the pit on page 12.

The range of plant remains in the sample is exceptional for Roman London and presumably form part of ritual food offerings. Stone pine remains from London have so far been found only in small quantities and mainly in waterlogged deposits from riverside sites in the City and Southwark. City sites include several on the Thames waterfront, for example Regis House (Davis in prep b; see also Willcox 1977), and 1 Poultry (Davis in prep a) and Copthall Avenue (de Moulins 1990) both in the Walbrook Valley, while Southwark sites include Cotton's Wharf, Tooley Street (Giorgi in prep) and charred remains from Borough High Street (Gray-Rees in prep). This was presumably a high-status food, occurring only on sites with relatively affluent residents. These were from contexts associated with food consumption rather than religious offerings. While no other definite use of stone pine in religious ceremonies has been found in Roman London, their use in such rituals is confirmed by the presence of charred stone pine kernels along with other foods in 1st- to 3rd-century deposits from the Vestal Virgins complex in the Forum, Rome (Costantini & Giorgi 1989).

There is some evidence from London, in the form of branches and associated cones, for the introduction of stone pine to Britain in the Roman period (D Goodburn, pers comm) although it is unlikely that many trees would have reached maturity and be producing cones before the end of the 1st century AD, and the cone scales and nut shells found in this deposit are probably from cones imported from the Mediterranean area for food and ritual purposes. The presence of cone scales and nut shells in the same context suggests that complete cones were imported.

The date and almond also represent imported fruits. Almond has occasionally been recovered from Roman deposits, for example from 1 Poultry (Davis in prep a), although date has never previously been identified from Roman London. It has, however, been found in Roman Colchester (Murphy 1984). The figs may represent either imported or possibly homegrown fruit, and while fig seeds are frequently found in Roman deposits this is the first record of the actual fruit being found as preserved remains. All these fruits are high-status foods and may provide some indication as to the affluence either of the person being cremated or of those attending a graveside ritual (thus implying that the dead woman was rich).

The plant remains and animal bone from this feature are considered in full detail elsewhere (Giorgi et al in prep).

6

French and German summaries

Résumé

Des fouilles en 1996 et en 1997 à Great Dover Street, Southwark CTQ3275 7935 (MoL code GDV96) fournirent l'évidence importante des inhumations et des structures associées à un cimetière romain situé au bord de la route au sud-est de la ville. La strate supérieure de la géology naturelle (OA1) fut couverte d'une séquence romaine qui commença avec un terrain extérieur et un fossé (OA2) du 1er. siècle apr.J.-C., aligné du nord-ouest au sud-est. Le fossé indiquait probablement une route romaine (R1) interpretée comme une partie de Watling Street. Vers la fin du 1er. siècle apr. J.-C. un bâtiment (B1), dont les murs extérieurs sur les pieux, fut construit au bord du sud-ouest de la route, avec l'axe en angle droit avec la route. Ce bâtiment, dont les dimensions de 8.6m par 5m au moins, fut limité par une série de fossés en pleine campagne (OA3), peut-être une partie d'un systéme de champ contemporain.

Le bâtiment fut démonté et les fossés remblayés pour faire place à un cimetière établi pas plus tard qu'au milieu du IIe. siècle. Un bâtiment de maçonnerie (B2), dont les dimensions 8m par 8m, fut situé dans la partie au sud de la fouille principale et en retrait de la route qui se trouva à l'est. Le plan du Bâtiment 2 donne l'idée peut-être d'un temple ou d'un temple-mausolée avec un mur extérieur discontinu qui entoura une *cella* centrale avec un puits ou un fossé d'écoulement. Une pierre d'autel possible, aussi bien qu'au moins deux inhumations, furent trouvées entre les murs intérieurs et extérieurs.

Un petit nombre d'inhumations à 30m environ au nord (OA4) ont peut-être été contemporaines du Bâtiment 2. Un *bustum* associé contint les restes mortels incinérés d'une femme aussi bien qu'au moins neuf tazze de poterie, huit lampes de poterie et une collection exceptionelle des restes de plante, dont un grand nombre importé de la méditerranée, y compris les pignons, les amandes blanches et la première découverte à Londres des dates. Les images sur les lampes dépeignèrent Anubis et un gladiateur.

Trois structures additionelles de cimetière furent bâties au nord du Bâtiment 2, même plus proches à la route, entre le milieu du IIe. siècle et le milieu du IIIe. siècle. Tout au nord du Bâtiment 2 se trouva le cimetière muré (S1) qui fut probablement construit pendant que le Bâtiment 2 se servait encore d'un temple. La Structure 1, dont 11m par 9m environ, contint au moins quatre inhumations et une grande fondation centrale de maçonnerie qui fut peut-êtrela base d'une tombeau ou d'un mausolée. Au sud de la fondation centrale se trouva une plus petite fondation de rocaille qui fut probablement la base d'un autre monument. Au nord de la fondation centrale une amphore enterrée debout, qui contint un depôt de clous, fut probablement un réceptacle des libations aux morts. Une grande coupe au coin du sud-ouest de l'enclôture contint une inhumation où la tête avait été mise sur la poitrine après la putréfaction du corps. Une pomme de pin pignon sculptée et une corniche moulée dont toutes les deux probablement d'un ou d'autre de tombeaux, furent trouvées dans la rocaille du cimetière muré (C1). La Structure l se fit servir probablement un peu après la démolition du Bâtiment 2.

Le mur extérieur du cimetière muré fut en partie volé au milieu du IIIe. siècle ou plus tard.

Tout au nord du cimetière muré (S1) fut trouvé un mausolée possible (S2) qui peut venir ou avant ou après le cimetière. Les dimensions du mausolée furent 6m par 5.8m environ. Les contre-boutants extérieurs trouvés aux côtés du nord-ouest et du sud-est soutenaient peut-être un toit voûté, bien qu'il n'y avait aucune évidence de parement.

Un deuxième cimetière muré (S3) dont des dimensions 9m par 4m environ, se trouva plus au nord. Le mur extérieur entoura aussi une fondation centrale de silex lié du mortier,et quatre inhumations.

Un nombre d'inhumations et de crémations enregistrées à l'extérieur du cimetière, y compris une groupe de trois inhumations en calcaire trouvées au sud-ouest du mausolée S 2 et datées à la fin du IIe. siècle jusqu'au IIIe. siècle, furent contemporains du cimetière, c'est à dire datés du milieu du IIe. siècle jusqu'au milieu du IIIe. siècle.

Le cimetière au bord de la route, qui fut à sa plus grande étendue au début du IIIe. siècle, indique que la construction des mausolées pour les personnes de haut rang et d'autres structures d'inhumation suivit Watling Street jusqu'à un demi-kilomètre environ de la limite probable de la ville. La disposition des structures et l'absence des inhumations superimposées donnent l'idée que le cimetière contint longtemps des parcelles de sépulture réservées pour les familles riches.

Les structures étaient tombées en ruines à la fin du IIIe. siècle, bien qu'il y avait quelque évidence d'un cimetière pas entouré (OA5). En tout, 25 inhumations et cinq cremations furent enregistrées de toutes les phases du cimetière.

La route se fit servir aussi longtemps que le cimietière et peut-être plus longtemps. La tête sculptée d'un dieu barbu, peut-être une déité d'eau, fut mise à jour d'un fossé au bord de la route. Le fossé fut recreusé à la fin du IIIe. siècle mais fut encore ensablé à la fin du IVe. siècle.

L'activité après l'époque romaine consista en des puits creusés au moyen âge et entre le XVIIe. siècle et le XIXe. siècle. L'activité la plus récente enregistrée sur ce site fut au XIXe. siècle la construction en brique, y compris des puits ou des fossés d'écoulement, une cave et d'autres murs.

Les trouvailles de Great Dover Street ont élargi notre connaissance des cimetières de Londres romain et complètent l'étude majeure du cimetière romain à l'est de la ville principale (Barber & Bowsher 2000). Le premier but de ce volume, c'est de décrire les trouvailles de Great Dover Street plus que d'essayer de synthétiser l'archéologie d'inhumations de Londres romain.

Zusammenfassung

1996 und 97 wurde in 165 Great Dover Street, Southwark (TQ 3275 7935) (MoL Kode GDV96) bedeutendes Material aus Begräbnisstätten und bauliche Anlagen offengelegt, die zu einem römischen Straßenfriedhof südöstlich der Siedlung

gehörten. Die oberste geologische Schicht (OA1) wurde von einer römischen Sequenz überlagert, die mit einem offenen Bereich und einem von Nordwesten nach Südosten verlaufenden Graben (OA2) aus dem ersten Jahrhundert begann. Der Graben markierte wahrscheinlich eine römische Straße (R1), die als Teil der Watling Street interpretiert wird. Im späten ersten Jahrhundert wurde ein Gebäude (B1), dessen Außenwände auf Pfeilern standen, auf der Südwestseite der Straße mit der Längsachse senkrecht zur Straße errichtet. Dieses Gebäude maß wenigstens 8,6m mal 5m und grenzte zu beiden Seiten an eine Reihe von Gräben im offenen Land (OA3), die zur gleichen Zeit Teil eines Feldsystems gewesen sein mögen. Gebäude B1 wurde abgetragen und die Gräben eingefüllt, um einem Friedhof Platz zu *Great Dover Street Excavations* machen, der nicht später als Mitte des 2. Jahrhunderts angelegt wurde. Ein Steingebäude (B2) von *ca.* 8m mal 8m wurde im südlichen Teil der Hauptausgrabung, von der Straße aus nach Westen zurückgesetzt, ausgegraben. Die Anlage des Gebäudes mag auf einen Tempel oder ein Tempelmausoleum hinweisen, wobei die unterbrochene Außenwand um eine zentrale *cella* und einen Brunnen oder eine Sickergrube führte. Die Basis eines möglichen Altars sowie auch wenigstens zwei Körperbeisetzungen lagen zwischen der inneren und der äußeren Wand des Gebäudes.

Einige wenige Körperbestattungen, die 30m nördlich gefunden wurden (OA4), mögen zur Zeit von Gebäude B2 stattgefunden haben. Ein dazugehöriges *bustum* enthielt verbrannte Überreste einer Frau, wenigstens neun getöpferte tazza und acht Lampen, sowie eine außerordentliche Ansammlung von Pflanzenresten, von denen viele aus dem Mittelmeerraum stammen wie Pinienkerne, weiße Mandeln und der erste Fund Datteln in London. Bilder auf den Lampen zeigen Anubis und einen Gladiator.

Drei weitere Friedhofsbauten wurden nördlich von Gebäude B2 und noch näher an der Straße zwischen Mitte des 2. bis Mitte des 3. Jahrhunderts errichtet. Unmittelbar nördlich von Gebäude B2 lag ein mit einer Mauer umgebener Friedhof (S1), der wahrscheinlich noch zu Lebzeiten des Gebäudes B2 angelegt wurde. Er maß ungefähr 11m mal 9m, enthielt wenigstens vier Grabstätten und ein zentralgelegenes Fundament, auf dem ein Grab oder Mausoleum gestanden haben mag. Südlich von diesem zentral gelegenen lag ein Schotterfundament, auf dem wahrscheinlich ein anderes Denkmal gestanden hat. Nördlich des Zentralfundaments stand senkrecht eingegraben eine Amphore mit einer Lage Nägel im Inneren. Sie war vermutlich ein Trankopfergefäß für die Verstorbenen. In einem breiten Schnitt in der Südwestecke des eingefriedeten Teils befand sich eine Körperbestattung, wobei der Kopf nach Verwesung des Körpers auf die Brust gelegt worden war. Schotter innerhalb des Friedhofs S1 enthielt einen geschnitzten Kiefernzapfen und ein gegossenes Sims, die beide aus einem der Gräber stammen müssen. Friedhof S1 mag Gebäude B2 um einiges überlegt haben. Die Umfriedungsmauer des Friedhofs wurde in der Mitte des 3. Jahrhunderts oder später teilweise ausgeraubt.

Direkt nördlich des Friedhofs lag möglicherweise ein Mausoleum (S2), das entweder älter oder jünger als der Friedhof S1 war. Das Mausoleum maß *ca.* 6m mal 5,8m. Seine externen

Strebepfeiler im Nordwesten und Südosten könnten ein gewölbtes Dach gestützt haben, wenn auch keine Hinweise auf Schmuck überlebt haben.

Ein zweiter ummauerter Friedhof (S3) lag weiter nördlich und maß ca. 9m mal 4m. Die äußere Wand lag auch um ein zentrales Flint-Mörtelfundament und enthielt vier Körperbestattungen.

Eine Anzahl Körper- und Verbrennungsbeisetzungen, die außerhalb der ummauerten Friedhofsanlagen lagen, waren aber zur gleichen Zeit entstanden, das heißt zwischen der Mitte des 2. und der Mitte des 3. Jahrhunderts. Hierzu gehört auch eine Gruppe von drei mit Kreide eingefassten Gräbern aus dem späten 2. bis 3. Jahrhundert, die im Südwesten des Mausoleums S2 gefunden wurden.

Der Straßenfriedhof, der sein größtes Ausmaß im frühen 3. Jahrhundert erreichte, zeigt, daß sich die Bauten der Mausoleen für hochgestellte Personen und andere Begräbnisse von der Grenze der Siedlung über ungefähr einen halben Kilometer entlang der Watling Street erstreckten. Die Anordnung der Anlage und das Fehlen überschneidender Gräber weist darauf hin, dass der Friedhof über eine ansehnliche Zeit von reichen Familien für Privatbegräbnisse benutzt wurde.

Die Begräbnisanlagen verfielen am Ende des 3. Jahrhunderts, obgleich einiges darauf hindeutet, daß dieses Gebiet weiter als uneingefriedeter Friedhof (OA5) benutzt worden sein mag. Insgesamt und über alle Phasen des Friedhofs wurden 25 Körper- und 5 Verbrennungsbestattungen ausgemacht.

Die Straße wurde während der gesamten Lebensdauer des Friedhofs und vielleicht sogar darüber hinaus benutzt. Der geschnitzte Kopf eines bärtigen Gottes, möglicherweise einer Wassergottheit, kam aus einem spätrömischen Straßengraben, der im ausgehenden 3. Jahrhundert neu ausgegraben wurde, im späten 4. Jahrhundert aber wieder versandet war.

Die nachrömischen Aktivitäten bestanden aus Gruben, die im Mittelalter und vom 17. bis 19. Jahrhundert angelegt wurden. Die jüngste Bautätigkeit bestand aus verschiedenen Ziegelkonstruktionen einschließlich eines Brunnens, Sickergruben eines Kellers und anderer Wände aus dem 19. Jahrhundert.

Die Resultate der Ausgrabungen von Great Dover Street erweitern unsere Kenntnis über Londons römische Friedhöfe bedeutend und werden die Hauptstudie über römische Friedhöfe im Osten Londons (Barber & Bowsher 2000) wertvoll ergänzen. Das Hauptziel der vorliegenden Arbeit ist, die Funde in Great Dover Street zu beschreiben, nicht aber der Versuch Londons römische Bestattungsarchäologie zusammen zu fassen.

BIBLIOGRAPHY

Abbreviations

BAR   British Archaeological Reports
CBA   Council for British Archaeology
MoLAS   Museum of London Archaeology Service

Place of publication given for titles published outside the United Kingdom.

Alcock, J P, 1980 'Classical religious belief and burial practice in Roman Britain', *Arch J* 137, 50–85

Allason-Jones, L, 1989a *Ear-rings in Roman Britain*, BAR British ser 201

Allason-Jones, L, 1989b *Women in Roman Britain*

Allason-Jones, L, 1996 *Roman jet in the Yorkshire Museum*

Anderson, A C & Anderson, A S (eds), 1981 *Roman pottery research in Britain and north-west Europe*, BAR International ser 123, 249–56

Bailey, D M, 1988 *A catalogue of the lamps in the British Museum: 3, Roman provincial lamps*

Baldacci, P, 1969 'Patrimonium e Ager Publicus al tempo dei Flavi', *La parola de passato* 128, 353–7

Balsdon, J P V D, 1969 *Life and leisure in Ancient Rome*

Barber, B & Bowsher, D, 2000 *The eastern cemetery of Roman London: excavations 1983–1990*, MoLAS Monograph 4

Bass, W M, 1995 *Human osteology: a laboratory and field manual*, 4th ed, Missouri Archaeol Soc Special Paper 2

Béal, J-C, 1983 'Médaillons, anneaux et fusaioles gallo-romains en bois de cerf à Clermond Ferrand', *Bull Hist et Scient de l'Auvergne* 12, 370–86

Bentley, D & Pritchard, F, 1982 'The Roman cemetery at St Bartholomew's Hospital, London', *Trans London Middlesex Archaeol Soc* 33, 134–72

Berry, A C & Berry, R J R, 1967 'Epigenetic variation in the human cranium', *J Anatomy* 101, 361–79

Bird, J, Graham, A H, Sheldon, H & Townend, P, 1978 *Southwark excavations 1972–74*

Bird, J, Hassall, M & Sheldon, H, 1996 *Interpreting Roman London*

Black, E W, 1986 'Romano-British burial customs', *Arch J* 143

Booth, P, 1982 'A Romano-British burial from Mancetter', *Trans Birmingham & Warwickshire Archaeol Soc* 92, 134

Brailsford, J W, 1958 *Guide to the antiquities of Roman Britain*, British Museum

Brooks, S T & Suchey, J M, 1990 'Skeletal age determination based on the *os pubis*: comparison of the Acsàdi-Nemeskèri and Suchey-Brooks methods', *J Human Evolution* 5, 227–38

Brothwell, D R, 1981 *Digging up bones: the excavation, treatment and study of human skeletal remains*, 3rd ed

Charlesworth, D, 1971 'A group of vessels from the Commandant's house, Housesteads', *J Glass Stud* 13, 34–7

Clark, J (ed), 1995 *The medieval horse and its equipment*, Medieval finds from excavations in London 5

Clarke, G, 1979 *The Roman cemetery at Lankhills*, Winchester Studies 3, Roman and Pre-Roman Winchester, part 2

Conheeney, J, 2000 'Inhumation burials' in B Barber & D Bowsher, 277–96

Constantini, L & Giorgi, J, 1989 'The plant remains from the Regia-Vesta excavations 1988', Archive Report, unpub

Cool, H E M & Philo, C, 1998 *Roman Castleford: excavations 1974–85, vol 1: The small finds*, Yorkshire Archaeol 4

Cool, H E M & Price, J, 1995 *Roman vessel glass from excavations at Colchester, 1971–85*, Colchester Archaeol Report 8

Coulston, J C & Phillips, E J, 1988 *Corpus signorum imperii romani, Great Britain I.6, Hadrian's Wall west of the North Tyne, and Carlisle*, Oxford:

The British Academy

Cowan, C, 1992 'A possible *mansio* in Roman Southwark: excavations at 15–23 Southwark Street, 1980–86', *Trans London Middlesex Archaeol Soc* 43, 3–191

Cowan, C, Wheeler, L & Westman, A, in prep *Roman Southwark: the origins of the settlement*, MoLAS Monograph

Cox, M, 1989 'The human bones from Ancaster', Ancient Monuments Laboratory Report 93/89, English Heritage

Crummy, N, 1983 *The Roman small finds from excavations in Colchester 1971–9*, Colchester Archaeol Report 2

Crummy, N, Crummy, P & Crossan, C, 1993 *Excavations of Roman and later cemeteries, churches and monastic sites in Colchester 1971–88*

Dangréaux, B & Desbat, A, 1988 'Les Amphores du dépotoir Flavien du Bas-de-Loyasse à Lyon', *Gallia* 45, 115–53

Davies, B J, Richardson, B & Tomber, R S, 1994 *The archaeology of Roman London, 5: a dated corpus of early Roman pottery from the City of London*, CBA Research Report 98

Davis, A, in prep a 'The plant remains', in J Hill & P Rowsome

Davis, A, in prep b 'The plant remains from Regis House'

De Moulins, D, 1990 'Environmental analysis', in *The upper Walbrook in the Roman period* (ed C Maloney), 85–115

Detsicas, A, 1983 *The Cantiaci*

Dilly, G & Mahéo, N, 1997 *Verreries antiques du Musée de Picardie*, Amiens

Down, A & Rule, M, 1971 *Chichester excavations 1*, Chichester Civic Soc Excavation Committee

Driver, J C, 1982 'Medullary bone as an indicator of sex in bird remains from archaeological sites', in B Wilson et al

Drummond-Murray, J & Thompson, P, in prep *Roman Southwark, the early settlement: excavations for the Jubilee Line Extension 1992–1999*

Farwell, D E & Molleson, T I, 1993 *Poundbury, vol 2: The cemeteries*, Dorset Nat Hist Archaeol Soc Monograph 11

Ferembach, D, Schwidetzky, I & Stloukal, M, 1980 'Recommendations for age and sex diagnosis of skeletons', *J Human Evolution* 9, 517–49

Finnegan, M, 1978 'Non-metric variation of the infracranial skeleton', *J Anatomy* 125, 23–37

Follmann-Schulz, A B, 1988 *Die römischen Gläser aus Bonn*, Cologne

Giorgi, J, in prep 'The plant remains in Roman Southwark'

Giorgi, J, Wardle, A & Mackinder, A, in prep *The contents of a probable bustum from Great Dover Street, Southwark, London*

Goethert-Polaschek, K, 1977 *Katalog der römischen Gläser des Rheinischen Landesmuseums*, Trier, Mainz am Rhein

Goethert-Polaschek, K, 1985 *Katalog der römischen Lampen des Rheinischen Landesmuseums*, Trier

Graham, A H, 1978 'Swan Street/Great Dover Street', in J Bird et al, 473–97

Grant, M, 1967 *Gladiators*

Gray-Rees, L, in prep 'The plant remains from the Jubilee Line Extension'

Greene, K, 1979 *Report on the excavations at Usk, 1965–76: the pre-Flavian fine wares*

Greep, S, 1994 'Antler roundel pendants from Britain and the north-west Roman provinces', *Britannia* 25, 79–97

Greep, S, 1998 'The bone, antler and ivory artefacts', in H E M Cool & C Philo, 267–84

Hall, J, 1996 'The cemeteries of Roman London: a review', in J Bird et al, 57–84

Hammerson, M, 1978 'Excavations under Southwark Cathedral', in *London Archaeol* 3, 206–12

Harden, D B, 1947 'The glass', in C F C Hawkes & M R Hull, 287–307

Harman, M, Molleson, T I & Price, J, 1981 'Burials, bodies and beheadings in Romano-British and Anglo-Saxon cemeteries', *Bull British Museum Nat Hist Geol* 35,145–88

Harris, E & Harris, J R, 1965 *The oriental cults in Roman Britain*, Études Préliminaires aux Religions Orientales dans l'Empire Romain 6, Leiden

Hatt, J J, Parruzot, P & Roes, A, 1955 'Nouvelles contributions à l'étude de médaillons et pendentifs en corne de cerf', *Revue Arch de l'Est et du Centre-Est* 6, 249–54

Hawkes, C F C & Hull, M R, 1947 *Camulodunum: first report on the excavations at Colchester 1930–1939*, Soc Antiq London Research Committee Report 14

Henig, M, 1984 *Religion in Roman Britain*

Henig, M, 1993 *Corpus signorum imperii romani, Great Britain I.7, Roman sculpture from the Cotswold Region*, Oxford: The British Academy

Heyob, S K, 1975 *The cult of Isis among women in the Graeco-Roman world*

Hill, C, Millett, M & Blagg, T, 1980 *The Roman riverside wall and monumental arch in London*, London Middlesex Archaeol Soc Special Paper 3

Hill, J & Rowsome, P, in prep *Excavations at 1 Poultry, vol 1: The Roman sequence*, MoLAS Monograph ser

Hillson, S, 1986 *Teeth*

Hoffman, J, 1979 'Age estimation from diaphyseal lengths: two months to twelve years', *J Forensic Science* 24, 461–9

Howe, M D, Perrin, J R & Mackreth, D F, 1980 *Roman pottery from the Nene Valley: a guide*, Peterborough City Museum Occasional Paper 2

Isings, C, 1957 *Roman glass from dated finds*, Archaeologica Traiectina 2

Jessup, R F, 1959 'Barrows and walled cemeteries in Roman Britain', *J Brit Archaeol Assoc* 3rd ser 22

Johns, C, 1996 'Isis, not Cybele: a bone hairpin from London', in J Bird et al, 115–18

Jones, C E E, 1986 'Roman glass', in R Whytehead, 86–8

Kaye, W J, 1914 'Roman and other triple vases', *The Antiquary* 50, 172–7, 223–6, 290–4

Lakin, D, in prep 'The Roman Tower at Shadwell: a reappraisal', Britannia

Lantier, R, 1929 *La Verrerie*, Musée des Antiquités nationales, Paris

Leibundgut, A, 1977 *Die römischen lampen in der Schweiz*, Berne

LIMC, 1997 *Lexicon Iconographicum Mythologiae Classicae, VIII, Thespiades-Zodiacus, supplementum*, Zurich and Dusseldorf

Loeschcke, S, 1919 *Lampen aus Vindonissa*, Zurich

Lyne, M A B & Jefferies, R S, 1979 *The Alice Holt/Farnham Roman pottery industry*, CBA Research Report 30

MacGregor, A, 1985 *Bone, antler, ivory and horn*

McKinley, J I, 1984 'Cremations: expectations, methodologies and realities', in C A Roberts et al, 65–76

McWhirr, A, Viner, L & Wells, C, 1982 *Romano-British cemeteries at Cirencester: Cirencester excavations 2*

Manning, W H, 1985 *Catalogue of the Romano-British iron tools, fittings and weapons in the British Museum*

Marsden, P R V, 1961 'Report on recent excavations in Southwark and Bermondsey', *Trans London Middlesex Archaeol Soc* 20, part 4

Martin, T S, 1997 'Two Roman ceramic spouted vessels from Essex', *Essex Archaeol Hist* 28, 281–2

Meates, G W, 1979 *The Lullingstone Roman villa, vol 1*

Meindl, R S & Lovejoy, C O, 1985 'Ectocranial suture closure: a revised method for the determination of age based upon the lateral anterior sutures', *Am J Phys Anth* 68, 57–66

Millett, M, 1979 'The dating of Farnham (Alice Holt) pottery', Britannia 10, 121–37

Monaghan, J, 1987 *Upchurch and Thameside Roman pottery: a ceramic typology* for northern Kent, first to third centuries AD, BAR British ser 173

Murphy, P, 1984 'Carbonised fruits from Building 5' and 'Charred cereals from Building 45, Room 6', in Excavations at Lion Walk, Balkerne Lane and Middlesborough, Colchester, Essex (ed P Crummy et al), Colchester Archaeol Report 3, 40, 108

Newstead, R, 1914 'The Roman cemetery in the Infirmary Field, Chester', Chester Annals Archaeol & Anthropol 6, 121–67

Niblett, R, 1999 The excavation of a ceremonial site at Folly Lane, Verulamium, Britannia Monograph 14, 70

Ortner, D J & Putschar, W G J, 1981 Identification of pathological conditions in human skeletal remains, Smithsonian Institute

Peacock, D P S & Williams, D F, 1986 Amphorae and the Roman economy: an introductory guide

Perring, D, 1991 Roman London

Perring, D & Roskams, S, with Allen, P, 1991 The archaeology of Roman London, 2: The early development of Roman London to the west of the Walbrook, CBA Research Report 70

Phenice, T W, 1969 'A newly developed visual method of sexing the os pubis', Am J Phys Anth 30, 297–302

Philpott, R, 1991 Burial practices in Roman Britain: a survey of grave treatment and furnishing AD 43–410, BAR British ser 219

Powers, R, 1988 'A tool for coping with juvenile human bones from archaeological excavations', in W J White, 74–8

Price, J, 1977 'Roman unguent bottles from Rio Tinto (Huela) in Spain', J Glass Stud 19, 30–4

Price, J, 1982 'The glass jar', in P Booth, 134

Price, J, 1987 'Glass from Felmongers, Harlow in Essex: a dated deposit of vessel glass found in an Antonine pit', in Annales du 10e Congrès de l'Association Internationale pour l'Histoire du Verre, Amsterdam, 185–206

Rackham, D J, 1995 'Skeletal evidence of medieval horses from London sites', in J Clark, 169–74

Rayner, L J, Seeley, F J, Symonds, R P & Tomber, R S, 1995 London research priorities for Roman pottery, MoLAS, unpub

RCHME (Royal Commission on the Historical Monuments of England), 1928 An inventory of the historical monuments in London, 3: Roman London

Resnick, D & Niwayama, G, 1988 Diagnosis of bone and joint disorders, 2nd ed

Rielly, K, 2000 'The animal bone', in B Barber & D Bowsher, 366–8

Rielly, K, in prep 'The animal bones', in B Yule

Rinaldi Tufi, S, 1983 Corpus signorum imperii romani, Great Britain, I.3, Yorkshire, Oxford: The British Academy

Roberts, C A, Lee, F & Bintliff, J, 1984 Burial archaeology: current research, methods and developments, BAR British ser 211

Rogers, J & Waldron, T, 1989 'Infections in palaeopathology: the basis of classification according to most probable cause', J Arch Science 16, 611–25

Rogers, J & Waldron, T, 1995 A field guide to joint diseases in archaeology

Rösing, F W, 1983 'Sexing immature human skeletons', J Human Evolution 12, 149–55

Shepherd, J D, 1998 The Temple of Mithras, London, English Heritage Archaeol Report 12

Shepherd, J D, 2000 'The glass', in B Barber & D Bowsher, 355

Stead, I M & Rigby, V, 1986 Baldock, the excavation of a Roman and pre-Roman settlement, 1968–72

Sundick, R L, 1978 'Human skeletal growth and age determination', Homo 39, 297–33

Symonds, R P, 2000 'The pottery', in B Barber & D Bowsher, 340

Symonds, R P & Tomber, R S, 1991 'Late Roman London: an assessment of the ceramic evidence from the City of London', Trans London Middlesex Archaeol Soc 42, 59–99

Symonds, R P & Wade, S M, 1999 Colchester archaeological report 10: the Roman pottery from excavations in Colchester, 1971–86

Thorpe, W A, 1935 English glass

Toynbee, J M C, 1986 The Roman art treasures from the Temple of Mithras, London, London Middlesex Archaeol Soc Special Paper 7

Tran Tam Tinh, V, 1972 Le Culte des divinités orientales en Campanie

Trotter, M & Gleser, G C, 1952 'Estimation of stature from long bones of American whites and negroes', Am J Phys Anth 10, 463–514

Trotter, M & Gleser, G C, 1958 'A re-evaluation of estimation of stature based on measurements of stature taken during life and long bones after death', Am J Phys Anth 16, 79–123

Turcan, R, 1966 Les Sarcophages romains à représentations dionysiaques, Paris

Turcan, R, 1996 The cults of the Roman Empire (trans A Neville)

Tyers, P & Marsh, G, 1978 'The Roman pottery from Southwark', in J Bird et al, 533–82

Ubelaker, D H, 1984 Human skeletal remains: excavation, analysis, interpretation, Smithsonian Institute

Vago, E B & Bona, I, 1976 Die Gräberfelder von Intercisa; der spätrömische südostfriedhof, Budapest

Vertet, H, 1969 'Vases a médaillons d'appliqué', Gallia 27, 93–133

von den Driesch, A, 1976 A guide to the measurement of animal bones from archaeological sites, Peabody Mus Bull 1, Cambridge, Mass.

von den Driesch, A & Boessneck, J A, 1974 'Kritische Ammerkungen zur Widerristhöhenberechnung aus Längenmassen vor-und frühgeschichtlicher Tierknochen, Säugetierkundliche Mitteilungen 22, 325–48

Waldron, T, 1994 Counting the dead: the epidemiology of skeletal populations

Webster, P, 1981 'The feeding cup: an unusual samian form', in A C Anderson & A S Anderson, 249–56

Wheeler, R E M, 1930 London in Roman times, London Museum Catalogues, no. 3

Wheeler, R E M & Wheeler, T V, 1936 Verulamium: a Belgic and two Roman cities, Soc Antiq London Research Committee Report 11

White, W J, 1988 Skeletal remains from the cemetery of St Nicholas Shambles, London Middlesex Archaeol Soc Special Paper 9

Whytehead, R, 1986 'The excavation of an area within a Roman cemetery at West Tenter St, London E1', Trans London Middlesex Archaeol Soc 37, 23–124

Wiedemann, T, 1992 Emperors and gladiators

Willcox, G, 1977 'Exotic plants from Roman waterlogged sites in London', J Arch Science 4, 269–82

Williams, R J & Zeepvat, R J, 1994 Bancroft: a late Bronze Age/Iron Age settlement, Roman villa and temple mausoleum, vol 1

Wilson, B, Grigson, C & Payne, S (eds), 1982 Ageing and sexing animal bones from archaeological sites, BAR British ser 109

Wilson, C A, 1973 Food and drink in Britain

Witt, R E, 1971 Isis in the Graeco-Roman world

Young, C J, 1977 Oxfordshire Roman pottery, BAR 43

Yule, B, in prep Roman Southwark, development in the north-west quarter: excavations at Winchester Palace, MoLAS Monograph

INDEX

Compiled by Susanne Atkin

Page numbers in **bold** refer to illustrations.

altar base 10
amphorae 58
  Gauloise, in upright position in S1
    14, **17**, 29, 51, **51**
  from roadside ditch 53, **55**
amulet see pendants
animal bones 64–5
  chicken (in burials) 12, 21, 45, 64
  corvid 12
  horse 32, 64–5
antler objects see pendants; toggle
Arcadia Buildings, Silvester Street/Great
    Dover Street 4
  medieval ditch 4
  pipe kiln 4
  road 4, 7, 24, 32
  timber buildings and metalworking 4
architectural evidence for structures
    30–1
Areas 1 and C–H 1

Baldock (Herts), lamps and cup 28
bead, glass 50
Billingsgate bath-house, pottery 55–6
Bishopsgate, glass vessel 47
Bonn (Germany), glass 44
Borough High Street 32, 59, 65
bracelets, copper-alloy 29, **49**, 50
Braxells Farm (Hants), tiles 61
brick 6, 10, 14, 15, 19, 21, 30, 57, 59;
  see also opus spicatum
brickearth 2, 5
bridge, Roman 2
British Museum
  glass bottle 42
  lamp 28, 33
  relief of woman in combat 28
brooches, copper-alloy 29, 42, 49
Building 1, timber 7, 8–9, **8**, **9**, 10
  (table 2), 59
Building 2 see temple-mausoleum
Burial 1 [b1] see bustum
Burial 2 [b2] 13, **14**, 37–8, **37**, 64
  glass 13, 38
Burial 3 [b3] 13, 24
Burial 4 [b4] 13–14
  'DISH' 38, 64
Burial 5 [b5] 14
Burial 6 [b6] 14
Burial 7 [b7], and chalk 14, 26, 29
Burial 8 [b8] 15–16, **15**, **17**, 22, 26, 29,
    38, **39**, 64
  decapitation post-mortem 15, **17**, 6,
    29
  glass bottle and jar 38, **39**
  pottery 22, 29, 38, **39**
  tile 59
Burial 9 [b9] **15**, 16, 38
Burial 10 [b10] **15**, 18, 22, 27, 38, 59
Burial 11 [b11] **15**, 18–19, 22, 27, 40, 59
Burial 12 [b12] **15**, 18–19, 22, 27, 40, 59,
    64
Burial 13 [b13] 19, 24, 40
Burial 14 [b14], in stone-lined cist 19,
    26, 29, 40, **40**
Burial 15 [b15] 19, 22, 40, 59
Burial 16 [b16] 19, 21, 40
  hobnails 19, 30, 40
Burial 17 [b17] 19, 22, 40, **41**
  on chalk in wooden coffin 19, 26, 29, 40
  pottery 19, 22, 40, **41**
Burial 18 [b18] 19, 27, 40–1, 64
  glass 41

hobnails 19, 40
Burial 19 [b19] 19, 41, **41**, 64
  pottery 19, 41, **41**
Burial 20 [b20] 19, 41
Burial 21 [b21] 19, 41–2, 64
  brooch 29, 42
  glass 19, 42
  pottery 19, 41–2
Burial 22 [b22] 19–20, **21**, 27, 42–3, **42**,
    64
  glass 42
  glass counter 42
  hobnails (shoes) 30, 43
  pottery 20
Burial 23 [b23], neonate 20, **21**, 27, 43
Burial 24 [b24] 20, 43
  pottery 20, 43
Burial 25 [b25], with chalk packing **18**,
    21, 26, 27, 29, 43, **43**, 64
  glass 43
  glass disc (gaming counter or
    pendant) 21, 30, 43, **46**
Burial 26 [b26], with chalk packing 21,
    26, 27, 29, 44–5
  chicken bone 21, 45, 64
  glass pyriform flask 21, 44–5, **44**
  jet pin 21, 29, **44**, 45
  nails 21
  rickets 27, 64
  shoes (staining from hobnails) 21, 30,
    45
  stone 59
Burial 27 [b27], with chalk packing **18**,
    21, 26, 27, 29, 45
  'DISH' 27, 64
Burial 28 [b28] 21, 22, 45–7
  glass 21, 46–7, **46**
  pottery 21, 22, 29, 45–6
  sandstone (flooring) 21, 30, 60
  tile flakes 59
Burial 29 [b29] 24, 27, 47, **48**
  pottery 24, 47, **48**
Burial 30 [b30] 24, 26, 48
  pottery, with graffiti 24, 29, 48
burial goods 26, 29–30, 32
  probably displaced 25, 48–51
burials 32, 33–48
  catalogue 52
  OA4 10–14, 22
  outside S1–S3 19–22, **20**, 22
  see also cremation burials; inhumation
    burials
bustum [b1] 10–13, 22, 27–8, 32, 33–7,
    34
  plant remains 11–12, 32, 65–6
  see also lamps; tazze

Caerleon (Gwent), lamp 34
Cardinal Bourne Street 4
cemetery (roadside) 9–23
  and its wider context 31–2
  population 26–7
  late Roman (Period 4) and unenclosed
    (OA5) 24
  see also walled cemetery, Structure 1
    and Structure 3
chalk (burials)
  grave packing 21, 26, 27, 29
  used in grave 14, 19, 26, 29
chalk objects see tessera
Chaucer House, Tabard Street 4
Chester (Cheshire), Infirmary Fields,
  glass flask 44

Chichester (W Sussex), lamp 34
child burials 26, 27
cinerary urns, glass 6, 27, 46–7, **46**
  glass square jar used as 27, **49**, 50
Cirencester (Glos) 26
  carved god 62
  glass bottle 44
cist, stone (and ?tile) see Burial 14
coffins, wooden 26, 29
coins 19, 22
  to pay Charon's fee 29
Colchester (Essex)
  almond 66
  beakers 47
  glass 43
  Maldon Road, glass bottle 45
  offerings of lamps 28
  pottery 40
  tettinae 49
copper alloy see bracelets; brooches
cornice mouldings, limestone 14, **17**, 30,
    31, 62–3, **63**
counters
  glass [from b2] 42
  glass disc as gaming counter or
    pendant [b25] 21, 30, 43, **46**
cremation burials 2, 13, 19, 20, 24, 26,
    27–9, 31, 40, 43, 45, 47, 48, 52, 63; see
    also bustum

decapitation post-mortem 15, **17**, 26
dental hygiene 27, 37, 38
Deverell Street, cremation burials 2
disc (gaming counter or pendant), glass
    21, 30, 43, **46**
'DISH' 27, 38, 45, 64
ditches/ditch system 4, 7, 22; see also
    field boundary ditches; Watling Street

eastern cemetery 2, 27, 29
  bracelet 50
  chicken bone 45
  children 26
  footwear 30
  hairpins 45
  horse bones 65
  lower jaws 26
  stature 64 (table 16)
Ewer Street, glass bottle 42
eyots 1–2

Falmouth Road/Great Dover Street,
    inhumation burials 2
family groupings 26, 27
field boundary ditches 2, 7, 8–9
figurine, pipeclay, post-medieval 25
finial see stone pine cone finial, carved
  flints
    as building material (knapped) 30, 59
    prehistoric 2, 4
funerary rites, burial practice and belief
    27–32

gaming counter (disc) see counters
geology 1–2
gladiators, female 28; see also lamps
glass
  burial goods 29
  from burials 13, 14, 19, 21, 37, 38, 41,
    42, 43, 44–5, 46–7
  jars **46**, 47
  molten, in bustum 13, 28
  ovoid bottle 38, **39**, 44
  phials (with inscription) 42, **46**, 47
  pyriform flask 21, 44–5, **44**
  square-sectioned vessels **46**, **49**, 50
  urn 46–7, **46**
  see also cinerary urns; counters;
    window glass
gold traces, from ?textile 37
graphic conventions 4
Guildhall Yard, cullet deposit 47

Harlow, Felmongers Lane, 'Airlie' cup 43
head of bearded river god, limestone 22,
    23, 30, 31, 61–2, **61**
hobnails 19, 21, 25, 30, 40, 43, 45
hone, stone 52
'Horsemongerland' 2
human bones 12, 24, 26–7, 63–4

inhumation burials 2, 4, 18–19, 26, 29,
    31, 52, 64; see also chalk; cist
iron objects 30; see also nails
Isis cult 28

jet see pin

Kentish ragstone 6–7, 9, 10, 14, 16, 30,
    59
Kent Street (Tabard Street) 2

lamps [in b1], ceramic 12–13, **13**, 27,
    28–9, 32, 33–7, **34–6**
  Anubis 12, 13, 28, 32, 33–4, **35**
  displaced burial goods 28, 48, **49**
  fallen gladiator 12, 28, 32, 33, **35**
  Firmalampen 13, 28, 35–7, **36**

Lankhills, Winchester 26, 27
Little London (Hants), tiles 61
Lombard Street, lamp 33
Lullingstone (Kent) 30, 31

Mansell Street 2, 47
marking-out ditch see Watling Street
mausoleum, Structure [2] **15**, 16, 18, **18**,
    22, 24, 31, 59
  ?tiled roof 30
  tufa block from ?vault 16, 30, 60
  see also temple-mausoleum; tower
    mausoleum
Moorgate Street, bone hairpin as Isis 28
Mucking (Essex) 28

nails, iron
  in amphora 14, 51
  in cremation burial 13
  from inhumation burials (coffins) 14,
    24, 26, 29
non-burial contexts, artefacts from 51–2

Old Kent Road 2
Open Area 1 (natural) 5
Open Area 2 (Area 1), open land and
    marking-out ditch for road 5–7, 8, **8**,
    10, 59
Open Area 3 (open land and field
    ditches) 5, 7, **8**, 9, 10 (table 2)
Open Area 4
  burials [b1–b7] 10–14, **11**, 37–8 (see
    also bustum)
  burials outside Structures S1–S3 [b13–
    b28] 19–22, **20**, 22, 40–7
  opus signinum 59
  other features 21–2
  see also wells
Open Area 5, unenclosed cemetery area
    23, 24, 31
Open Area 6 25
opus signinum 13, 19, 24, 30, 59, 60
  flooring 18
opus spicatum brick 7, 10
osteoarthritis 27, 40, 45, 64 (table 17)

parentalia, festival of the dead 51
pendants
  antler (amulet) 29, **49**, 50–1
  glass disc (or gaming counter) 21, 30,
    43, **46**
Period 1 (natural) 5
Period 2 (early land use) 5–9, **6**, **8**, 10
    (table 2)
Period 3 (roadside cemetery) 9–23;
  see also mausoleum (S2); Open Area 4;
    temple-mausoleum (B2);

walled cemetery (S1, S3)
Period 4 (Open Area 5) **23**, 24
    pottery 53–7
Period 5 (Open Area 6) 25
phallus 29, 51
pin (?shroud pin), jet 21, 29, **44**, 45
pine cones see plant remains; stone pine
    cone finial
pits
    square (OA4) 21
    wood-lined 7, **8**
plant remains 65–6
    almond 12, 66
    cereal grains 12
    charcoal 12
    date 12, 66
    figs 12, 66
    stone pine (cones and scales) 12, 28,
        65–6
plaster, painted 59
Poitiers (France), glass 45
pottery
    broken, in burials 29
    burial goods 29
    decoration codes 59
    fabric codes 58
    for cremation burials 27, 29
    form codes 58
    from inhumation burials 29
    from roadside ditch (Period 4) 53–7
    ware codes 59
    Alice Holt Farnham 54–5, **55**, 56
        in cremation burial, with graffiti
        [b30] 24, 29, 48, **49**
    Black-burnished (-type) ware 29, 38,
        43, 46, 55, **55**, 56, 58
    Central Gaulish White ware see lamps
    Colchester White ware 5
    Cologne Colour-coated ware 10
    Colour-coated ware 45
    Early Roman Sandy B ware 5
    grog-tempered 54, **55**
    Highgate 'B' ware 5
    Highgate 'C' ware 41
    Lyon Colour-coated ware 5
    Lyon ware lamp 48
    Moselkeramik 46
    Nene Valley Colour-coated ware 19,

29, 40, 47, 53–4, **54**, 55
    Oxfordshire Red Colour-coated 53,
        54, 55
    Oxfordshire wares 53, **54**, 55
    Oxidised ware 46, 54, 58 (see also
        tettina)
    Portchester 'D' ware 54, **54**
    prehistoric 2, 4
    (reduced) Sand-tempered ware 46, **54**
        (and see below 'votive' vessel)
    Thameside Kent Black-burnished-type
        ware 29, 46, 52
    Verulamium Region Coarse White-
        slipped ware 41–2, 46
    Verulamium Region White ware 38, 46,
        54, **54** (see also tazze)
    'votive' vessel, Sand-tempered ware 21,
        29, **49**, 51–2
    see also amphorae; lamps; tettina
Poultry, lamp 33
Poundbury (Dorset)
    burials 26
    painted plaster in mausolea 30
prehistoric, channel, flints and pottery
    2, 4
Purbeck marble slab 24, 30, 60

quarry pits 7, 24
quern, stone 52

Radlett (Herts), tiles 21, 60
Reigate (Surrey), tile kilns 60
Reigate stone 9, 10, 16, 30, 31–2, 59
Rephidim Street 4
rickets 27, 64
Road 1 see Watling Street
Rome (Italy), Forum 65
rubbish pit, late medieval 25

St Bartholomew's Hospital 26, 27
St George's Church 32
sandstone, flooring 21, 30, 60
Shadwell 'signal tower' or tower
    mausoleum 31
Sheepen (Essex), glass flask 44
shoes 21, 29–30; see also hobnails
Silvester Buildings, Silvester Street 4
Spitalfields, mausoleum structures 31

stature 26–7, 64 (table 16)
stone
    as building material 31–2, 59–60
    carved and moulded 22–3, 30, 31
    see also cornice mouldings; head of
        bearded river god; hone; Kentish
        ragstone; Purbeck marble slab;
        quern; Reigate stone; sandstone;
        stone pine cone finial; tessera
stone pine see plant remains
stone pine cone finial, carved limestone
    (?Caen) 14, **17**, 23, 30, 31, 62, **62**
Stone-by-Faversham (Kent), mausoleum
    16, **19**
Structure 1 see walled cemetery
Structure 2 see mausoleum
Structure 3 see walled cemetery
structures, architectural evidence 30–1, **31**
Swan Street/Great Dover Street 4

Tabard Street (formerly Kent Street) 1, 2
    Chaucer House 4
    inhumation burials and burial goods 2,
        31
tazze (VRW) 12–13, **13**, 27, 28, 29, 32, **34**,
    37
temple-mausoleum (Period 3, Building 2)
    9–10, **11**, **12**, 22, 31, 32, 59
    associated well 9–10, **12**, 22
    reconstruction 10, **31**
    see also Burial 6; Burial 7
tessera, chalk 24, 31
tettina, Oxidised ware 16, **18**, 29, 48–9
textual conventions 4
tile (roof tiles; wall tiles) 6, 10, 14, 15, 19,
    21, 24, 30, 57, 59
    fabrics 60–1
    flue tiles 19, 24
    imbrices 30
    north-west Kent 6, 7, 10, 13, 21, 60
    Radlett 21, 60
    Reigate kilns 60
    tegulae 19, 21
    tileworking, reworking (flakes) 19, 21,
        30, 57
toggle, antler 15, 50
Tooley Street, pottery flagon 28
topography 1–2
tower mausoleum 31

Trinity Square, inhumation burials 2
tufa block 16, 30, 60

veneer see Purbeck marble slab
Verulamium, tazze 37
'votive' jar see under pottery

walled cemetery, Structure 1 (S1) 14–16,
    15, **16**, **17**, 22, 24, 31
    amphora 14, **17**, 29, 51, **51**
    brooch 29, 49
    inhumation burials 14–16
    roof tile and brick 14, 15, 59
    stone 14, 32, 59–60
    see also amphorae; cornice mouldings;
        stone pine cone finial; tettina; toggle;
        window glass
walled cemetery, Structure 3 (S3) **15**,
    18–19, 22, 24, 30, 31
    coin 19
    flint 30, 59
    inhumation burials 18–19, 24, 27
        (see Burials b10–b12, b29)
    opus signinum 18, 19, 24, 30, 59
    plinth 18
    pottery 19, 20, 21
    tile and brick 19, 59
    wooden structure 18
watching brief WB1 1, **3**, 21–2
    Firmalampe 48
watching brief WB2 1, **3**, 7, 22
watching brief WB3 1, **3**, 7
watching brief WB4 1, **3**, 7
Watling Street (Road 1) 2, 7, **7**, 8, 9, 22,
    23, 24, 26, 32
    marking-out ditch (OA2) 5–7, **6**, 8
    roadside ditch(es) 4, **6**, 7, **7**, **11**, **20**, 22,
        23, 24, **25**, 30, 32
    horse bones 64–5
    pottery (Period 4) 32, 53–7
wells 4
    in OA3 7, **8**
    stone-lined, associated with temple-
        mausoleum (Period 3) 9–10, **12**, 22
    timber (OA4) 21, 22, 30, 60
West Tenter Street, glass jar 47
Winchester Palace, horse bones 64
window glass 14, 30, 52